Epic Soccer Stories

Inspiring True Tales of Legends, Underdogs, Pioneers & Rising Stars That Teach Confidence, Resilience, Teamwork & Love of the Game

Dylan Ambrose

YEARN MORE PUBLICATIONS

Thank You for Joining the Epic Soccer Journey!

We're so glad you picked up *Epic Soccer Stories* — part of the **Epic Sports Series**, where real-life tales of teamwork, grit, and leadership inspire young readers to dream big and play bold.

As a special thank you, we'd love to give you a **free Epic Basketball Activity Sampler** — packed with fun mazes, puzzles, trivia, and more!

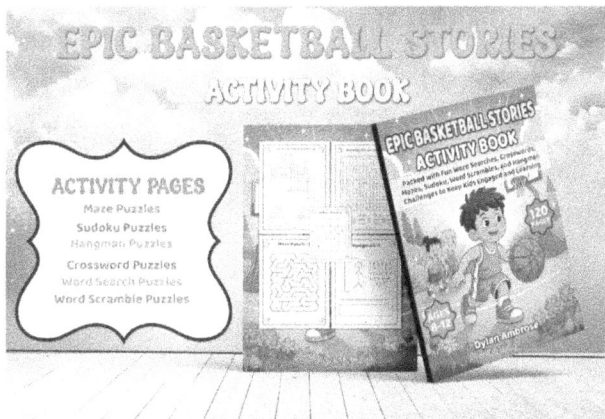

Grab your bonus in our website by clicking the link or scanning the QR Code: https://pages. yearnmorebooks.com

By signing up, you'll be first in line for future **Epic Sports Series** releases — think inspiring stories for **baseball, football, hockey, tennis, and more**!

To your next adventure,
Dylan Ambrose
Epic Sports for Kids | YearnMoreBooks.com

CONTENTS

1. Introduction   1

2. Chapter 1: How Soccer Began (and Why It Stuck Around)   5

    1.1 Ancient Kicks: The World's First Soccer Players

    1.2 England Changes Everything Forever

    1.3 The Incredible Story of When Girls Were Banned (But Played Anyway!)

3. Chapter 2: What Legends Teach Us   13

    2.1 Pelé's Never-Give-Up Spirit

    2.2 Maradona's Magic on the Field

    2.3 Zidane's Grace Under Pressure (and Learning from Mistakes)

    2.4 Christine Sinclair's Barrier-Breaking Journey

    2.5 Abby Wambach's Courage and Leadership

    2.6 Homare Sawa and Japan's Midfield Magic

4. Chapter 3: Today's Soccer Superstars   35

    3.1 Kick after Kick: Messi's Big Dreams

    3.2 From Kicks to King: How Ronaldo Rose to the Top

    3.3 Lightning Feet: Kylian Mbappé's Superpower

    3.4 Alex Morgan's Playbook for Success

3.5 Scoring Superstar: Sam Kerr's Soccer Magic

5. Chapter 4: Rising Stars to Watch   57
    4.1 From Boots to Brilliance: Jude Bellingham's Rise
    4.2 Strong Steps: How Alphonso Davies Beat the Odds
    4.3 Flair on the Field: Meet Jadon Sancho
    4.4 Trinity Rodman's Power: Speed, Strength, and Spirit
    4.5 Salma Paralluelo's Spark: Born to Be a Champion

6. Chapter 5: The Women Who Changed the Game   75
    5.1 Crowned in Cleats: Marta's Soccer Journey
    5.2 Ada's Voice, Ada's Victory
    5.3 Big Dreams, Far Travels: Meet Asisat Oshoala
    5.4 From Seoul to the World: Ji So-yun's Soccer Adventure
    5.5 Megan's Message: Play Hard, Speak Loud
    Make Your Best Pass Yet

7. Chapter 6: More Than a Game: Life Lessons from the Pitch   95
    6.1 When You Lose, Learn
    6.2 Winning Together
    6.3 Playing Fair, Playing Proud
    6.4 Train Hard, Play Bold
    6.5 Eyes on the Goal
    6.6 Teammates, Challengers, and Change

8. Chapter 7: One Game, Many Cultures   115
    7.1 Soccer Around the World
    7.2 Africa's Joyful Game
    7.3 Soccer with South American Swagger
    7.4 European Strategy and Tradition
    7.5 Rising Stars in Asian Soccer

9. Chapter 8: Goals, Glory, and Grit   133
    8.1 Brazil 1970: When Soccer Became Poetry
    8.2 Denmark 1992: The Ultimate Last-Minute Heroes

8.3 Aguero 2012: The Goal That Stopped Time

8.4 Leicester City 2015-16: When Dreams Defied Reality

8.5 Making Your Own Iconic Moment

10.   Chapter 9: Funny Moments on the Field   147

9.1 Famous Bloopers: When Soccer Gets Silly

9.2 Pranks and Fun: Locker Room Legends

9.3 Goal Celebrations: Dancing Into Soccer History

11.   Chapter 10: Behind Every Great Player   157

10.1 Legendary Coaches: The Game Changers

10.2 Mentors Who Changed Everything

10.3 Parents: The Ultimate Cheerleaders

10.4 Who Inspires You?

12.   Chapter 11: Behind the Scenes in a World Cup City   171

11.1 Stepping Into a Stadium of the Future

11.2 When the World Comes to Your City

11.3 Where Dreams Take the Field

13.   Conclusion   185

Also by Dylan Ambrose

14.   References   189

INTRODUCTION

It was a blazing hot December day in Varadero, Cuba, 77°F and sunny, the kind of weather that invites you to the beach, but not that afternoon. Instead of lounging by the shore, we were shoulder-to-shoulder with tourists from all over the world, packed into a resort conference room.

Everyone was glued to the giant screen, French fans, Argentinian fans, and Canadians like us. For those two hours, it didn't matter where we were from. We were all transported to Qatar, watching the **2022 FIFA World Cup Final** unfold in real time.

Argentina vs. France. Messi vs. Mbappé. It wasn't just a match, it was an epic showdown. Every goal sets off cheers or groans. When Argentina pulled ahead, their fans exploded in celebration. But then Mbappé answered, once, twice, three times, and the French fans roared back to life. They leapt from their seats, waving flags and shouting, "*Allez les Bleus!*" After 120 minutes of heart-stopping action, the score was tied 3–3. Then came the penalties.

Each shot brought silence, then eruptions. And when Gonzalo Montiel scored the final goal to win it 4–2 for Argentina, the room became a wave of flags, hugs, and tears. Argentinian fans rolled on the floor in celebration, sobbing and laughing. Even the French fans clapped, stunned by what they'd just witnessed.

Lionel Messi sank to his knees as the final whistle blew. His teammates swarmed him in a tidal wave of joy. After *five* World Cups, after years of carrying his nation's hopes, he had finally done it: He was finally a World Cup champion!

That's what soccer does. It brings people together and creates unforgettable memories. Messi had won almost everything, but the World Cup always slipped away. He never gave up, and on that night in Qatar, he finally held the one trophy he'd dreamed of since childhood.

That's the power of *never giving up*. That's the heart of the game. And that's what this book is all about.

What Makes This Book Special

This isn't just another soccer book filled with stats and scores. You'll meet real soccer legends like **Messi** and **Ronaldo** alongside incredible heroes like **Christine Sinclair** and **Abby Wambach**, players who prove that with heart, determination, and teamwork, anyone can achieve **greatness**.

Get ready to laugh out loud! We've packed this book with **hilarious bloopers**, epic goal celebrations gone wrong, and moments that prove even world-class players are human, too. These funny stories show that soccer is meant to be enjoyed, not just endured.

Every story teaches powerful life lessons about **resilience, teamwork, and believing in yourself**. These aren't preachy lessons. They're woven into exciting tales of players who faced real challenges, made tough choices, and emerged stronger. Just like *you* can.

We celebrate the beautiful diversity of soccer, featuring heroes from **every corner of the globe** with different countries, cultures, and backgrounds. You'll especially love our **female soccer superstars** who shattered barriers and inspired millions of girls to chase their dreams fearlessly.

As a bonus, get an exclusive peek behind the scenes as **Toronto** prepares for the **2026 FIFA World Cup**! Ever wonder what happens when your city becomes the center of the soccer universe? You'll see how an entire city transforms for the biggest soccer celebration on Earth.

Your Journey Starts Here

The best part? This book doesn't just tell you about these amazing players. It invites you into their world. You'll find **reflection questions** and **fun challenges** that help you connect their journeys to your own life. What would YOU do in their cleats?

So grab your favorite snack, find a comfy spot, and dive in. Get ready to be inspired, laugh, and discover that soccer is more than just a game. It's a way to connect, learn, and shine.

Let's kick off this journey together!

CHAPTER 1: HOW SOCCER BEGAN (AND WHY IT STUCK AROUND)

"Football is an art, like dancing. It requires whole-hearted concentration."

— Arsène Wenger, iconic coach of England's Arsenal FC

The Secret That Shocked Everyone

What if I told you that soccer was once BANNED for half the world's population? What if I said that ancient players sometimes faced life-or-death consequences for losing a match? Or that one simple rule change in 1863 accidentally created two completely different sports?

Sounds impossible, right? Well, get ready to have your mind blown. The story of soccer is packed with plot twists, surprising heroes, and moments that changed everything. From emperors watching ancient Chinese matches to women secretly playing in muddy fields for fifty years, this isn't the boring history lesson you might expect.

Have you ever wondered where soccer, the game we all love, actually began? It might surprise you to learn that soccer's roots run incredibly deep, deeper than most people think. Long before Messi or Ronaldo were scoring goals, people all over the world were playing ball games that looked a lot like soccer. And these games weren't just about kicking a ball around, they were about bringing people together, creating stories, and making history.

Ready to uncover the wildest secrets in soccer history? Let's dive in!

1.1 Ancient Kicks: The World's First Soccer Players

China: Where It All Started (Over 2,000 Years Ago!)

Close your eyes and imagine you're in ancient **China**, standing in front of the emperor's palace. There's a crowd gathering, and you can feel the excitement in the air. What's happening? The world's first soccer match!

They called their game **Cuju** (which means "*kick ball*"), and it was way harder than today's soccer. Imagine trying to kick a leather ball stuffed with feathers through a tiny hole in a net, while your emperor was watching every move! Talk about pressure. Miss the target, and you might end up in serious trouble. Score, and you'd be celebrated as a hero.

The coolest part? These ancient Chinese players developed incredible foot skills because they HAD to be precise. Every touch mattered. Sound familiar? That's the same feeling you get when you're trying to thread a perfect pass between defenders!

Greece and Rome: When Soccer Met Wrestling

While Chinese players were perfecting their foot skills, the **Greeks** had their own wild version called **Episkyros**. Imagine soccer, but players could use their hands, feet, shoulders, basically whatever worked! It was like organized chaos, and it was awesome.

The **Romans** loved this Greek game so much they created their own version called **Harpastum** to train their soldiers. These weren't just games, they were boot camp! Roman generals believed that if you could handle a crazy ball game with your buddies, you could handle anything on the battlefield.

Mesoamerica: The Most Intense Ball Game Ever

But wait, here's where the story gets really wild. Across the ocean in **Central America**, people were playing ball games that would make your toughest match look like a friendly kickabout.

Players had to get a heavy rubber ball through stone hoops mounted high on walls, without using their hands OR feet! They could only use their hips, shoulders, and elbows. And here's the part that'll blow your mind: they believed the gods were watching every single move. Some historians think the losing team faced consequences so serious that...well, let's just say missing a penalty kick suddenly doesn't seem so bad!

The Amazing Connection: All these ancient games, separated by thousands of miles and hundreds of years, shared something magical: the pure *joy* of controlling a ball. That feeling when you pull off the perfect touch or score an amazing goal? Kids have been experiencing that exact same rush for literally thousands of years!

1.2 England Changes Everything Forever

1863: The Year That Created Modern Soccer

Fast-forward to **1863** in **England**. Think of smoky factory towns, busy cobblestone streets, and workers who finally had some free time on weekends. Soccer was everywhere, but it was total chaos, every town, every school, every neighborhood had completely different rules!

In one place, you could pick up the ball and run with it. In another, that would get you kicked out of the game. Some places had goals the size of garage doors, others had tiny targets. It was like trying to play a video game where the rules kept changing every five minutes!

Then something game-changing happened that would affect every soccer player for the rest of time.

A group of people got together and formed the **Football Association (FA)**, and they did something revolutionary: they wrote down the first official rulebook. But here's the funny part: not everyone was happy about it.

The Great Split: When the FA said "*no more picking up the ball with your hands,*" some players basically said, "*Are you kidding me? That's the best part!*" They loved grabbing the ball and running with it so much that they refused to give it up. So what did they do? They said "*Fine, we'll make our own sport!*" And that's how rugby was born.

One meeting, one rule change, two completely different sports that millions of people play today. Talk about a decision that changed the world!

1872: The Match That Started Everything

ENGLAND vs. SCOTLAND
THE FIRST INTERNATIONAL MATCH
1872

This is the historic moment: **England vs. Scotland**, the very first international soccer match ever played. After 90 minutes of action, the final score was... 0-0.

Sounds boring? It was actually HUGE! This wasn't just a soccer game, it was proof that two different countries could come together and play by the same rules. That simple 0-0 draw launched *international soccer* as we know it. Every **World Cup**, every international tournament, every time your national team plays, it all traces back to that one match in 1872.

Soccer Goes Global

Here's where the story gets really exciting. **British** sailors and traders were traveling all over the world, and everywhere they went, they brought soccer with them. But something magical happened: each place that discovered soccer didn't just copy it, they made it their own.

Brazilian kids started playing barefoot on beaches, developing the fancy footwork and creativity we still see today. African children made balls from rags and scraps, creating a style full of improvisation and joy. **Argentina** fell head-over-heels in love with the beautiful game and developed their own passionate, technical approach.

Soccer became like a universal language that everyone could speak, but with their own special accent. And that's part of what makes it so beautiful today!

1.3 The Incredible Story of When Girls Were Banned (But Played Anyway!)

Get ready for a story that'll make you both angry and inspired at the same time.

1921: The Most Ridiculous Ban in Sports History

In 1921, the Football Association in England made one of the worst decisions in sports history. They actually BANNED women from playing soccer on official pitches. Their reason? They claimed soccer was "*too rough*" for women.

Can you believe that? The same sport that kids play in playgrounds all over the world was supposedly too dangerous for half the population. It's hard to imagine now, but back then, many people actually believed this nonsense.

The Heroes Who Refused to Quit

But here's where the story gets amazing: women didn't care about the ban. They didn't give up their love for soccer just because some people said they couldn't play. Instead, they got creative.

They played in muddy fields behind schools. They set up games in empty lots. They organized matches in parks where no one was looking. For FIFTY YEARS, women kept soccer alive in secret, proving that when you truly love something, no rule or ban can stop you.

These weren't just rebels, they were heroines. Every time they laced up their boots and stepped onto those makeshift fields, they were fighting for the rights of every girl who would come after them.

1971: Freedom at Last!

When the ban was finally lifted in **1971**, something incredible happened: women's soccer didn't just come back, it exploded! Players like **Mia Hamm** became superstars in the 1990s, showing the world what they'd been missing. In **2011**, **Homare Sawa** led Japan to an amazing World Cup victory that had people crying tears of joy.

And those claims that soccer was "too rough" for women? Players like **Megan Rapinoe**, **Alex Morgan**, and thousands of others have completely demolished that ridiculous idea. They've proven that *passion, skill, and determination* have absolutely nothing to do with whether you're a boy or a girl.

The Ultimate Comeback: Today, women's soccer is one of the fastest-growing sports in the world. Every girl who steps onto a soccer field today is continuing the legacy of those brave pioneers who refused to take "*NO*" for an answer.

Your Soccer DNA: You're Part of This Amazing Story

Here's something incredible to think about: every single time you kick a ball, you're continuing a story that began with ancient Chinese emperors, survived English factory towns, traveled around the globe with explorers and traders, and was kept alive by women who refused to quit.

You're not just playing a game, you're part of a 2,000-year-old tradition of people who discovered that kicking a ball around brings pure joy, connects communities, and proves that the simplest ideas often become the most powerful.

From ancient ceremonial courts to modern World Cup stadiums, one thing has never changed: that magical moment when you strike the ball perfectly and everything else disappears. The crowd, the pressure, your worries, it all fades away, and it's just you and the ball. That's your soccer DNA kicking in, connecting you to every player who's ever felt that same incredible feeling!

Think about it: when you nutmeg someone in the playground, you're experiencing the same thrill that made Chinese emperors cheer 2,000 years ago. When you score that perfect goal, you're feeling the same joy that made those brave women play in secret fields for fifty years. You're part of something much bigger than just a game, you're part of a family that spans the entire world and reaches back through all of history.

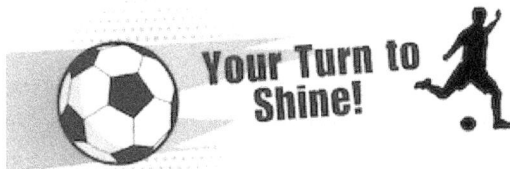

Your Turn to Shine!

Your Soccer Story Timeline

Can you trace your soccer DNA?Soccer has traveled through centuries — from ancient Chinese emperors to secret women's matches in muddy fields. Now it's your turn to join the journey!
Activity: Create your own "Soccer Story Timeline"!
    1. **Draw a timeline starting 2,000 years ago.**

    2. **Add these historic milestones from the chapter:**

- Cuju in ancient China

- Episkyros in Greece

- Harpastum in Rome

- Formation of the Football Association in 1863

- Women's ban in 1921

- Women's soccer explosion after 1971

    3. **Now add YOUR story!**

- When did you first kick a ball?

- What's your first soccer memory?

- Who inspires you today?

- What's your biggest soccer dream?

Bonus: Decorate your timeline with small drawings, emojis, stickers, or colors that represent each event.

Coming Up Next: Get ready to meet the legends who took this ancient game and became household names around the world. These aren't just famous players, they're ordinary kids who grew up to change soccer forever. Their stories will show you that with enough passion and determination, anything is possible!

CHAPTER 2: WHAT LEGENDS TEACH US

PELÉ   MARADONA   ZIDANE

SINCLAIR   USA WAMBACH   SAWA

You have to fight to reach your dream. You have to sacrifice and work hard for it.

— Lionel Messi

W hat makes a soccer player legendary? Is it scoring jaw-dropping goals, winning trophies, or dazzling the crowd with incredible moves? Sure, those moments are exciting, but true legends are remembered for something even greater: their *character*, *spirit*, and the way *they inspire people* on and off the field.

In this chapter, we'll step into the shoes of six amazing soccer heroes whose stories go far beyond highlight reels. You'll discover how **Pelé** taught the world to keep going, even when it feels impossible. You'll see **Maradona** turn pressure into pure magic, and watch **Zidane** stay composed when the stakes are sky-high (and learn from his one famous mistake). You'll meet **Christine Sinclair**, who broke barriers and lifted a nation, and **Abby Wambach**, whose fearless leadership lit up every game. And don't miss **Homare Sawa**, who led Japan's midfield with quiet strength and determination.

These aren't just stories about scoring goals. They're about grit, grace, and daring to believe in yourself. As you read, think about how each player's journey holds lessons you can use in your own life, whether you're playing on a field, working with a team, or facing your own challenges. Let's dive in and meet these living legends!

2.1 Pelé's Never-Give-Up Spirit

PELÉ

O Rei (The King)

DID YOU KNOW?

Pelé scored over 1,280 goals in his career, the most by any professional soccer player in history! 🏆

Position: Forward ⚽
Country: Brazil ⚽

Growing up in Brazil, **Pelé** had nothing but a dream and a sock full of rags to kick around. In his childhood, he didn't have fancy shoes or a proper ball. But he certainly had determination! Pelé loved soccer more than anything else. He played every chance he got, dribbling around obstacles life threw at him. Soccer was his ticket to a brighter future.

Life wasn't easy for Pelé. He faced many setbacks on his way to the top. Some people told him he was *too young* or *too small* to make it big. Others didn't even give him a chance. But Pelé didn't let rejection stop him. Instead, he worked even harder. His dedication paid off when he joined **Santos FC** at just *fifteen years old*. Can you imagine being that young and already playing for a top club? Not many people get to do that!

Pelé's rise didn't stop there. At seventeen, he got a chance to shine on the world stage during the **1958 World Cup**, the biggest soccer tournament in the world, held every four years. Most teenagers would be nervous, but not Pelé. He scored *six goals* in the tournament, leading **Brazil** to victory. People called him a soccer prodigy. His determination was clear when he recovered from injuries to help Brazil win the **World Cup** *again* in **1962** and **1970**. Pelé was unstoppable.

Pelé's influence went beyond the soccer field. He used his fame for good, advocating for sports as a tool for social change. He encouraged kids everywhere to play soccer and pursue their dreams, no matter their circumstances. As a **UNICEF Goodwill Ambassador**, someone who helps the United Nations organization that protects children worldwide, Pelé supported causes that helped children and communities in need.

Pelé's legacy continues to inspire young players today. Take **Neymar**, for instance. He grew up idolizing Pelé and dreamed of following in his footsteps. Neymar has often spoken about how Pelé's story motivated him to push through challenges and reach his goals. In Brazil, countless young athletes see Pelé as a symbol of hope and possibility.

Timeout for Your Thoughts: What Would You Do?

Ever felt like giving up when things got tough? Pelé didn't. Even when people told him he was too skinny, too poor, or just not good enough, he kept going, and looked where that took him!

Think back to a time when you faced a challenge.

1. What happened?

2. How did you react?

3. Looking back, what could you do differently if it happened again?

Now imagine you're the hero of your own sports story. Write a short scene:

1. Describe your challenge as if it were a big moment in a soccer match.

2. Show how you'd handle it next time, using Pelé's grit and determination.

3. End with your "winning goal": What lesson did you learn?

Remember that even champions like Pelé stumbled before they soared. Your story matters too.

2.2 Maradona's Magic on the Field

DIEGO MARADONA

El Pibe de Oro (The Golden Boy)

DID YOU KNOW?

★ Maradona captained Argentina to win the 1986 World Cup, scoring or assisting 10 of Argentina's 14 goals in the tournament!

Position: Attacking Midfielder
Country: Argentina

A soccer player can dance with the ball as if it were part of him. That's how **Diego Maradona** played. His creativity and flair made him a legend. Maradona was famous for making the impossible look easy, especially during the **1986 World Cup** in **Mexico**.

During that tournament, Maradona created two of soccer's most memorable moments in the same game against England. First came the controversial "**Hand of God**" goal, where he punched the ball into the net with his fist, which is completely against the rules. The referee didn't see it, and the goal counted. Maradona later said "*a little with the head of Maradona and a little with the hand of God.*" People still debate this moment today!

But just four minutes later, Maradona scored what many call the "**Goal of the Century**." He dribbled past half the English team, weaving in and out like a magician on the field, before sliding the ball into the net. It was pure artistry. This goal showed his incredible skill and creativity, the kind that left everyone speechless.

Maradona's creativity wasn't just about fancy tricks. It changed games. When he played for **Napoli** in **Italy**, he led them to their first-ever championship victories. His inventive play inspired his teammates and fans alike. With Maradona, you never knew what he'd do next, and that's what made watching him so exciting. He had moves like the *Maradona turn*, where he'd spin past defenders so quickly they'd be left wondering where he went.

Today's players still look up to Maradona for inspiration. **Lionel Messi**, another Argentine great, often cites Maradona as an influence. Messi's dribbling has the same grace and creativity. Players everywhere try to emulate Maradona's style, especially creative midfielders who want to control the game like he did. They study his moves, hoping to capture even a bit of his magic on the field.

Maradona's impact went beyond soccer. His style transcended sports and became a cultural phenomenon. People admired his ability to create something amazing out of nothing. His play was like art, full of expression and joy. Fans around the world saw him as a symbol of creativity and passion. Even today, when people talk about Maradona, they remember his genius with a smile.

Your Turn to Shine!

Try the Maradona Turn

Ready to add a sprinkle of magic to your game? Find a buddy and some open space. It could be your backyard, the park, or even the playground.

Here's how to channel your inner Maradona:
1. Start with the ball at your feet.

2. As your friend comes to challenge you, gently drag the ball back with one foot.

3. Then spin your body around, using your other foot to keep the ball close.

4. Burst away like you've just escaped a defender in the final seconds of a match!

It might feel wobbly or weird at first, and that's okay! Even Maradona practiced moves over and over before he made defenders look silly.

Remember that soccer isn't just about scoring goals or winning medals. **Maradona taught us it's also about *art*, *flair*, and showing the world your *style*.** Next time you're out there, don't be afraid to try something new. Twist, spin, dance with the ball, and who knows? You might create your very own moment of magic that people will remember.

2.3 Zidane's Grace Under Pressure (and Learning from Mistakes)

ZINEDINE ZIDANE

Zizou

DID YOU KNOW?

★ Zidane scored two headers in the 1998 World Cup Final, leading France to its first-ever World Cup victory on home soil!

Position: Midfielder ⚽
Country: France

Think about a soccer game with everything on the line. The crowd is roaring, and the pressure is intense. That's when **Zinedine Zidane** usually stepped onto the field like he was born for the moment. In the **1998 World Cup Final**, he played with ice in his veins. Calm as ever, Zidane scored two headers and helped lead **France** to victory on home soil. Even during tough **Champions League** matches, Europe's biggest club tournament, Zidane kept the same steady focus: no flinching, no panicking, just cool, controlled brilliance.

How did he usually do it? He had mental tricks that helped him stay sharp:

1. **Visualization**: Before games, Zidane pictured himself doing well, scoring, passing, staying in control. This mental practice helped him stay ready for anything.

2. **Staying Cool**: When opponents tried to throw him off with trash talk or rough plays, he usually kept his composure. He didn't let anyone get into his head.

But even legends aren't perfect. In his final game, the **2006 World Cup Final**, Zidane made a mistake that taught the world an important lesson. After an opponent said something hurtful to him, Zidane lost his temper and headbutted the player. He was sent off in his last-ever game. Later, Zidane said he regretted his action, even though he was angry about what was said. This moment reminds us that even the calmest players are human, and managing our emotions is something we all have to work on.

Zidane's usual composure made him a great leader. As captain of the French national team, he led by example. His teammates trusted him because he almost always gave his best, especially when things got tough. When Zidane became a coach, that same level-headed style brought success. He led **Real Madrid** to multiple Champions League victories, showing that focus and confidence work both on and off the field.

Young players today still look up to him. **Paul Pogba**, a star for France, often talks about how much Zidane inspires him, not just for his skills but for how he usually stayed calm, focused, and kind under pressure, and for how he learned from his mistakes.

Your Turn to Shine!

Zidane's Focus Trick

Want to train your brain like Zidane? Here's a warm-up for your mind before your next game or test:

1. Close your eyes and breathe slowly.

2. Think of a time you did something awesome, like scoring a goal or solving a tough problem.

3. See it clearly in your mind: how it feels, sounds, and even what you're wearing.

4. Open your eyes and smile. Now you're ready.

Bonus Challenge: Think of a time you lost your temper. What could you do differently next time to stay calm like Zidane usually did? Remember, even legends make mistakes, it's how we learn from them that matters.

2.4 Christine Sinclair's Barrier-Breaking Journey

CHRISTINE SINCLAIR

Captain Canada

DID YOU KNOW?

⭐ Sinclair carried Canada's flag at the 2012 London Olympics closing ceremony, honoring her leadership and 6-goal performance that earned Canada the bronze medal. 🏆

Position: Forward ⚽
Country: Canada 🍁

In **Canada**, a young girl named **Christine Sinclair** picked up a soccer ball and didn't just kick it, she *booted* it with purpose. That moment marked the beginning of something incredible. Christine fell in love with soccer early and quickly made waves in her local leagues. With sharp *skills* and serious *determination*, she caught the attention of coaches and soon wore the Canadian jersey with pride.

Christine's rise wasn't just about scoring goals. It was about *changing the game for women* everywhere. As captain of the Canadian national team, Christine led with heart. She wasn't just any player, she was a leader who inspired her teammates to give their best. She stayed calm under pressure and lifted others with her energy and focus. Younger players looked up to her, learning from her wisdom both on and off the field. With Christine at the helm, Canada became a team the world had to take seriously.

And then came the record, unbeatable as of this writing. Christine became the *all-time leading goal scorer* in international soccer, for both men and women, with an incredible **190 goals**. That's more goals than anyone in history! But for Christine, each goal wasn't just a statistics. It was a message: *Women's soccer matters*. Her achievements sparked celebration across the world. Kids everywhere, especially girls, saw what was possible because of her.

But Christine didn't stop at greatness on the field. She knew that soccer was more than just a game, it was also a force for change. She spoke out for gender equality in sports, calling for equal pay and better opportunities for women. She challenged unfair systems and pushed for respect for all athletes, no matter their gender.

Off the field, Christine's mission continued. Through her foundation and community work, she helped girls chase their dreams just like she had. She made sure young female players had the support, equipment, and confidence they needed to thrive. For Christine, soccer was a tool for building bridges and breaking down barriers.

Through it all, she proved that being a great athlete also means being a great human. Her *leadership, grace,* and *determination* continue to inspire players around the world. In Canada and beyond, girls tie up their cleats and step onto the field thinking of Christine Sinclair, ready to make history in their own way.

So next time you're kicking a ball or watching a match, remember Christine. She's not just a soccer star, she's a *trailblazer* who helped change the game for good.

Your Turn to Shine!

Christine's Confidence Challenge

Christine Sinclair didn't just play soccer, she changed it. She stood up for what was right and showed the world that girls belong on the field, scoring goals and breaking records.

Want to tap into her kind of courage? Try this mini challenge:

1. Think of something you love doing, maybe it's soccer, art, music, or speaking up in class.

2. Write down one big dream you have for that activity. Don't hold back! Big dreams are allowed here.

3. Now write one small step you can take this week to move closer to that dream, like practicing for ten minutes a day, asking for help, or cheering someone else on.

4. Stand tall and say out loud: "*I belong here. I'm strong, and I can make a difference.*"

Just like Christine, you have the power to lead, inspire, and stand up for what matters. Whether you're on the field or off it, your voice counts. And who knows? Maybe one day, your story will help someone else chase their dream, too.

2.5 Abby Wambach's Courage and Leadership

ABBY WAMBACH

The Header Queen

DID YOU KNOW?

Wambach scored 184 international goals, and an incredible 77 of them were headers—more than any other player in soccer history!

Position: Forward ⚽
Country: United States

Abby Wambach charged toward the goal with power and purpose: fearless, fast, and unstoppable. She didn't just play soccer in the **USA**, she reshaped it. When she stepped onto the field during **World Cups** and **Olympics**, the entire stadium buzzed with energy. Her goals made headlines, her grit fired up the fans, and young players all over the country found a new reason to believe in their dreams.

Abby's signature move is the header. The ball flies through the air toward the goal, defenders scramble, and suddenly, THUD!, Abby's forehead connects with the ball, sending it rocketing past the stunned goalie. "*Did you see that?!*" kids would shout from the stands, jumping up and down. At 5'11", Abby towered over many defenders, and she used every inch of her height to her advantage. She threw herself into every play with total commitment, playing like every game was the most important one of her life. By the time she hung up her boots, she'd scored **184** goals for **Team USA**, a world record that stood until Canada's Christine Sinclair surpassed it. But here's what made Abby a true *legend*: she didn't just score goals, she turned every header into a work of *art*, and every moment on the field into an example of fearless *courage*.

Her courage made her a natural leader. As team captain, Abby didn't bark orders but she led by example. In high-stakes games, she stayed calm and focused, pushing her teammates to keep going, even when things got tough. Her leadership helped the team stay united, confident, and ready for anything. Players knew they could count on Abby to fight for every ball and never give up.

Her impact stretched far beyond the soccer pitch. She used her platform to champion social causes that mattered deeply to her. Abby spoke out for gender equality, standing up for equal pay and opportunities in sports. Her work to make things better didn't stop there. She advocated for LGBTQ+ rights and used her influence to make a difference in the world. Her courage in speaking out inspired many to do the same, showing that athletes can be powerful agents of change.

Abby's legacy proves that *courage* and *leadership* can change the game on the field and beyond. Through her goals, her strength, and her voice, Abby showed the world that you can play fiercely and stand up for what's right at the same time.

Your Turn to Shine!

Abby's Leadership Challenge

Think about a time you wanted to speak up but felt nervous. Maybe it was in class, during a game, or when something didn't feel fair. What would Abby do?

Try this:

1. Write down one thing you believe in, something that matters to you.

2. Now, list one small action you can take to support it. It could be encouraging a teammate, including someone who feels left out, or standing up for a fair rule.

3. Next time you're on the field or in a tough moment, take a deep breath, stand tall, and lead with heart just like Abby.

Practice Abby's Signature Header: Find a soft ball and practice gentle headers with a parent or coach. Remember: head the ball, don't let the ball head you! Start low and slow, focusing on using your forehead and keeping your eyes open.

Remember, being **brave** doesn't always mean being loud. It means **doing what's right even when it's hard**. That's real leadership.

2.6 Homare Sawa and Japan's Midfield Magic

HOMARE SAWA
The Golden Goddess

DID YOU KNOW?

Sawa played in six different FIFA Women's World Cups (1995–2015), the most by any player of her era, showing incredible skill and longevity.

Position: Midfielder
Country: Japan

Leading your team to a **World Cup** win for the *first* time in your country's history, that's exactly what **Homare Sawa** did for **Japan** in **2011**. As captain, she guided her team with skill and heart, proving that anything is possible. Sawa's role as a *playmaker*, the player who creates opportunities for teammates to score, was crucial. She made passes that left opponents stunned and created plays that seemed to come from nowhere. Her brilliance earned her both the *Golden Ball* as the tournament's best player and the *Golden Boot* for scoring the most goals, a double honor that proved she was truly legendary.

But Sawa's story isn't just about trophies. Her *perseverance* made her a legend. She joined **Japan's national team** when she was just *fifteen years old*, younger than most high school students! Over her career, she faced injuries and tough losses but refused to quit. Japan wasn't always seen as a top team, but Sawa believed in her squad. Her quiet, steady leadership showed that *teamwork* and *dedication* could overcome anything.

The **2011 World Cup** was especially meaningful because it came just months after a devastating earthquake and tsunami hit Japan. The team dedicated their victory to their country, and Sawa's leadership helped inspire a nation during a difficult time, turning soccer a symbol of *hope* and *resilience*.

Sawa's impact went far beyond the field. She lit a spark in girls all over **Japan** and across **Asia**. Many saw her success and thought, "*I can do that too.*" In 2011, she became the *first Asian player* to win **FIFA Women's Player of the Year.** That moment sent ripples through the soccer world and inspired even more girls to chase their dreams.

Why is Sawa a legend? She proved that soccer is about *smart play* and *selflessness*. She taught us that *quiet leadership* can be just as powerful as loud leadership. Her influence reaches far beyond Japan, touching players all over the world who admire her commitment and skill.

Your Turn to Shine!

Think Like a Playmaker

Want to play like Sawa? Grab a ball and a friend. Try this quick challenge:

1. Set up three passes that lead your partner to a clear shot or goal. Think ahead: Where should they be? Where should you be?

2. After each turn, talk it through. What worked? What could you try differently next time?

3. **Bonus Round**: Try to make a pass that surprises your friend in a good way, maybe behind them, to their side, or with perfect timing.

Playmakers like Sawa don't just pass, they think ahead. They see the big picture and help the whole team shine. Practice seeing the game from that angle, and you'll be leading in no time.

What We've Learned

As we wrap up this chapter on amazing soccer legends, think about what makes them special. Whether it's Pelé's never-give-up *determination*, Maradona's *creative magic*, Zidane's *composure* (and learning from mistakes), Sinclair's *barrier-breaking courage*, Wambach's *fearless leadership*, or Sawa's *quiet strength*, they've all shown us something valuable about soccer and life.

These legends teach us that:

- **Persistence pays off** (Pelé never gave up)

- **Creativity makes you special** (Maradona's artistic play)

- **Staying calm helps you succeed** (Zidane's focus, plus learning from mistakes)

- **Breaking barriers opens doors for others** (Sinclair's record-setting career)

- **Courage extends beyond the field** (Wambach's leadership and advocacy)

- **Quiet strength can be powerful** (Sawa's humble excellence)

Soccer has a way to inspire and bring people together. Each of these legends reminds us that true greatness goes far beyond what happens on the soccer field.

Next up, we'll meet today's rising stars, players who are making history right now and carrying forward the lessons these legends taught us!

CHAPTER 3: TODAY'S SOCCER SUPERSTARS

Kylian Mbappé

Sam Kerr

Lionel Messi

Alex Morgan

Cristiano Ronaldo

Success is no accident. It is hard work, perseverance, learning, studying, sacrifice, and most of all, love of what you are doing or learning to do.

—Pelé

S ome soccer stars become legends over time, but what about the heroes we're lucky enough to watch right now? This chapter is all about today's game changers, players whose talent, dedication, and fearless attitude have turned them into worldwide icons. They show us that greatness isn't about being perfect, it's about showing up, giving your best, and daring to dream big.

We'll follow **Lionel Messi**, a boy from Argentina whose love for the game and unstoppable spirit turned him into one of history's greatest. We'll see how **Cristiano Ronaldo** rose from humble beginnings to become a global superstar through sheer determination. You'll discover **Kylian Mbappé**'s blistering speed and fearless attitude, **Alex Morgan**'s playbook for staying sharp under pressure, and **Sam Kerr**'s magical way of scoring goals that leave fans breathless.

These modern-day heroes prove that confidence isn't something you're simply born with. It's something you build every single day. As you read their stories, think about the times you've had to keep pushing, learn something new, or work with your teammates. Get ready to be inspired, because these soccer stars show that with courage, dedication, and a little bit of magic, anything is possible!

3.1 Kick after Kick: Messi's Big Dreams

LIONEL MESSI

La Pulga (The Flea)

DID YOU KNOW?

Messi scored 7 goals in the 2022 World Cup!

Position: Striker

Country: Argentina

In the city of **Rosario, Argentina**, a small boy chased a big dream with a soccer ball at his feet. That boy was **Lionel Messi**. Life wasn't always easy for him. At age *eleven*, doctors diagnosed him with a growth hormone deficiency. This condition required expensive treatment for proper growth, a massive cost for his family. Even with this enormous challenge, Messi's family refused to give up. They sacrificed greatly, believing their young star would achieve greatness.

Then came a life-changing moment. At age *thirteen*, Messi made a huge move, leaving Argentina for Spain. This transformed his life and career forever. He joined **FC Barcelona**'s famous youth academy, **La Masia**. The move meant leaving his home, friends, and everything he knew behind. This significant step marked the beginning of a journey filled with determination and resilience. Just like he moved past defenders, he handled this transition and pressure with remarkable focus. When he debuted with Barcelona's senior team at age *seventeen*, everyone could see his incredible talent and resolve. Messi's journey shows that his unwavering commitment to pushing through tough challenges was as important as his natural skill.

Throughout his career, Messi collected trophies like kids collect trading cards, he just couldn't stop! He won a record **eight Ballon d'Or awards** (that's like being named the world's best player eight times!), **four Champions League titles**, **ten La Liga championships**, and shelves full of other prizes. But there was one trophy missing from his collection: the **World Cup**. Four times he tried, and four times he came so close he could almost touch it. *"Will Messi ever win the World Cup?"* fans wondered. Then, at age *thirty-five*, on his fifth try, he finally did it! In Qatar, Messi lifted the World Cup high above his head, proving that dreams come true when you refuse to quit.

Every time a young player steps onto the field, they can think of Messi. He started as a small kid with big dreams, proving that size doesn't determine greatness, *heart* does. If he can do it, so can *you*.

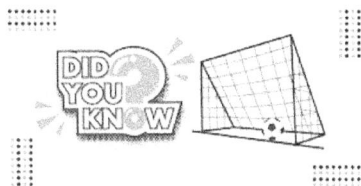

Messi's Secret Tribute

Every time Messi scores a goal, he points up to the sky. But do you know why? **He's saying "*thank you*" to his grandmother, Celia, who was his biggest fan!** She was the one who first took him to a soccer field when he was just four years old. When coaches thought little Messi was too small to play, Grandma argued with them until they let him join the team.

Sadly, she passed away when Messi was only 11 years old, before she could see him become a superstar. But Messi never forgot her love and support. That's why every goal celebration is really a message to heaven: "***This one's for you, Grandma!***"

Next time you watch Messi play, look for that special point to the sky, now you know the beautiful story behind it!

Your Turn to Shine!

Set Your Goal Challenge

Are you ready to train like a champion? Just like Messi didn't become great overnight, reaching your goal takes small steps, focused effort, and an unstoppable attitude. Here's how you can get started:

1. **Choose your goal.** Pick something you really want to improve. It could be learning a new soccer move, finishing a challenging book, or improving at math. Write it down: "My goal is to…"

2. **Break it down.** Think of three small steps you can take this week to get closer to your goal. These steps should be simple and doable.

Example Goals:
- Juggle the ball ten times.

- Practice five minutes a day

- Watch a how-to video

- Ask a coach or friend for help

Messi's story proves that success is not just about talent but also about *perseverance and persistence*. So whatever goal you choose, give it your all. The journey might be challenging, but what you achieve will be worth it.

3.2 From Kicks to King: How Ronaldo Rose to the Top

A vibrant and enthusiastic boy from the beautiful island of Madeira in **Portugal** had a huge dream and an even bigger heart, full of ambition. That boy is none other than **Cristiano Ronaldo**. From an early age, Ronaldo had an unshakeable belief in his potential to become the best soccer player in the world. However, success didn't stem purely from dreaming; it was his *relentless work ethic* that laid the foundation for his remarkable journey.

Ronaldo's training was legendary. He dedicated himself intensely to enhancing his physical attributes: running faster, leaping higher, and striking the ball harder than his peers. Furthermore, he devoted countless hours to gym workouts to ensure he maintained peak physical fitness, complementing the rigorous practice sessions that challenged and continuously sharpened his skills. This unstoppable spirit of *self-improvement* allowed him to shine brilliantly at every club he joined.

When he arrived at **Manchester United**, some critics disliked his flashy style and questioned his decisions. But Ronaldo showed exceptional mental strength. Instead of getting discouraged, he used criticism to elevate his game even further. He worked tirelessly to become a complete player, methodically improving his dribbling, passing, and goal-scoring to an elite level. His dedication paid off spectacularly. He eventually led Manchester United to numerous victories. Ronaldo's unrelenting attitude led to a historic triumph when he guided **Portugal** to their *first* **European Championship title** in **2016**. This monumental feat not only brought immense joy to his compatriots but also demonstrated his unparalleled persistence and tenacity, cementing his legacy in soccer history.

Ronaldo's remarkable influence transcends the boundaries of soccer. It's also about the profound way he connects with individuals worldwide. With millions of followers on social media platforms, Ronaldo offers glimpses into his multifaceted life, sharing workout routines, motivational messages, and personal moments with his fans. People around the globe admire him not solely for his extraordinary soccer prowess but equally for his *generous heart*. Through substantial donations to charitable organizations, supporting children in need, and endorsing various global causes, Ronaldo's kindness off the field inspires widespread admiration. It solidifies his status as a hero, not just for aspiring athletes but for countless individuals.

Ronaldo emerges as an ideal role model for anyone aspiring to turn their dreams into reality. Young enthusiasts worldwide strive to emulate his intense training regimen and unwavering discipline. They gain invaluable understanding from his example that realizing ambitions necessitates *consistent effort* and *steadfast commitment*. Beyond *skill* and *dedication*, Ronaldo advocates a *balanced lifestyle*. He speaks passionately about the importance of proper nutrition, maintaining fitness, and treating one's body with care. Through his exemplary lifestyle, he motivates others to adopt healthier habits, perfectly demonstrating the powerful link between physical well-being and lasting success.

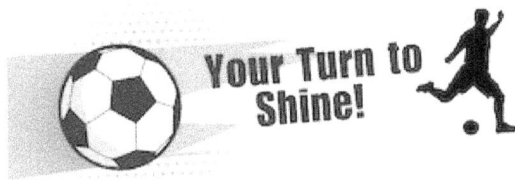

Try Ronaldo's Routine

Want to train like a soccer legend? Ronaldo didn't become one of the world's best by luck, he practiced consistently every single day. Now it's your turn to give his routine a try!

Your Daily Mini Routine:

1. **Stretch it out.** Loosen up your muscles so you don't get hurt. Try toe touches, arm circles, and lunges.

2. **Jumping jacks.** Do 2 to 3 minutes to get your heart pumping.

3. **Dribble practice.** Spend 15 minutes a day working on ball control. Set up cones or bottles and weave through them.

Keep a notebook or chart where you can track how many days in a row you stick to this plan. Watch yourself get stronger, faster, and more confident. **Ronaldo's success came from *showing up every day*, not just when he felt like it**. Whether you're training on the field or working diligently in school, his story reminds us that consistent effort beats raw talent when talent doesn't work consistently.

3.3 Lightning Feet: Kylian Mbappé's Superpower

KYLIAN MBAPPÉ
The Lightning Bolt

DID YOU KNOW?

⭐ **Mbappé became the first teenager since Pelé to score in a World Cup Final.** 🌍⚡

Position: Forward ⚽
Country: France 🇫🇷

In the lively streets of **Bondy, France**, a young boy named **Kylian Mbappé** was kicking a soccer ball around with friends. His love for the game showed in every move. At **AS Bondy**, his *speed* and *sharp instincts* were evident from the start. Coaches quickly saw he wasn't just quick, he could read the game and outsmart defenders with ease. It wasn't long before he joined **AS Monaco**'s youth academy, where his skills grew even sharper. Every match seemed to confirm what many already suspected: this kid was destined for greatness.

Mbappé's playing style is absolutely electric. He is lightning fast! In fact, he once reached a speed of *38 kilometres per hour* during a match, faster than most people drive in school zones! But speed isn't his only weapon. Mbappé's dribbling techniques are mesmerizing. He can zigzag through defenders like he's dancing on the field. It's almost like the ball is magnetized to his feet. This combination of velocity and creativity makes him a nightmare for any defender trying to stop him.

His impact on French soccer has been nothing short of magical. At just *nineteen* years old, Mbappé played a pivotal role in leading **France** to victory in the **2018 World Cup**, not only with his blistering speed and goals but also by consistently driving the attack and demonstrating composure under immense pressure. He became the *youngest* French player to score in a World Cup final, a testament to his ability to lead from the front and inspire a nation to believe in collective greatness. Kids everywhere started dreaming of following in his footsteps, hoping to wear the blue jersey of Les Bleus one day.

Off the pitch, Mbappé works tirelessly to give others a chance to chase their dreams too. Through his foundation, *Inspired by KM*, he helps provide sports programs and education to kids who don't have easy access to them. He often visits schools and youth centers, encouraging students to work diligently and stay curious. He believes every child, no matter where they're from, deserves a chance to succeed.

Mbappé's story isn't just about talent, but also about heart. He remains grounded, kind, and focused, regardless of the praise he receives. Fans love him not only for what he does on the field, but also for how he carries himself off it, with *humility* and *generosity*.

Speedometer Infographic

Get ready for a wild race! Here's a fun way to see just how speedy Kylian Mbappé is. We've lined him up against some of the fastest animals and vehicles on Earth. Who wins? Let's find out!

Speed Lineup (Slowest to Fastest):

1. Garden snail: 0.05 km/h
2. Running child (age 8–10): 13–18 km/h
3. House cat: 30 km/h
4. Kylian Mbappé: 38 km/h
5. Olympic cyclist: 70 km/h
6. Cheetah: 100–120 km/h
7. Race car: 300+ km/h

Mbappé might not beat a cheetah, but he definitely leaves most defenders in the dust! His top speed is faster than most kids can bike!

3.4 Alex Morgan's Playbook for Success

ALEX MORGAN

Captain Clutch

DID YOU KNOW?

Morgan scored a World Cup goal in just 12 seconds — one of the fastest ever!

Position: Forward
Country: United States

Alex Morgan wasn't born a soccer star. She became one by working intelligently, staying focused, and refusing to back down. As a kid, she loved the game so much that she would practice for hours, always chasing the ball with *determination* and *joy*. That drive took her all the way to the **University of California, Berkeley**, where she made a name for herself on the college soccer team. Her speed, strategic thinking, and goal-scoring power helped lead her team to significant victories and set the stage for what came next.

After college, Alex joined the **US Women's National Team**. She didn't waste a single moment. With every match, she proved she could hold her own among the best players in the world. Her quick feet, intelligent plays, and unstoppable energy helped the team dominate on the field. She trained intensively, stayed sharp, and continued to rise, no matter how tough things got.

Injuries tried to slow her down, but Alex always came back stronger. She pushed through the pain with grit and determination, resolved to keep playing the game she loved. Her training routine was intense, comprising sprints, drills, and strength workout but she refused to quit. That effort paid off spectacularly.

In **2019**, Alex helped lead the **US team** to another **World Cup victory**. As co-captain, she didn't just play, she also led. Her leadership, both on and off the field, inspired young players everywhere to believe in their own strength. That same year, she became one of the most vocal advocates in the fight for equal pay in soccer, standing up for fairness and respect for women athletes worldwide.

Alex's impact doesn't end when the game is over. She's also a *writer* and the *creator of The Kicks book series*, fun, exciting stories about a group of soccer players who support each other on and off the field. Through her books, Alex encourages kids to be *strong, stay kind, and chase their dreams.*

She's passionate about making sports more accessible and inclusive for everyone, and she works to ensure girls have the same opportunities as boys. Whether she's scoring goals, writing books, or speaking up for fairness, Alex shows what it means to be a true champion.

So next time you lace up your cleats or pick up a book, think about Alex's champion mindset. Remember that you can achieve great things too if you believe in yourself and work consistently.

Coach's Pep Talk: Your Own Champion Mindset!

Alright, champ, today you're thinking like Alex. Here's your game plan:

1. **Set a goal.** It could be anything: score a goal, run a little faster, or learn a new trick.

2. **Stick with it.** If it's tough, take a deep breath and keep going, champions don't quit.

3. **Help someone else.** A champion isn't just great at sports, they lift up their teammates, too.

Write or draw your **Champion Day** in the space below. What did you do? How did it feel?

GOALS *Planner*

QUOTE

SHORT TERM GOAL 1

(Start Date):   *(End Date):*

(Action Steps)   *(Notes)*

○ _____
○ _____
○ _____

SHORT TERM GOAL 2

(Start Date):   *(End Date):*

(Action Steps)   *(Notes)*

○ _____
○ _____
○ _____

SHORT TERM GOAL 3

(Start Date):   *(End Date):*

(Action Steps)   *(Notes)*

○ _____
○ _____
○ _____

⦿ TO START   ⊘ DONE   ⊖ DELAY   ⊘ STUCK   ⊗ CANCEL

3.5 Scoring Superstar: Sam Kerr's Soccer Magic

SAM KERR

Flying Matilda

DID YOU KNOW?

⭐ Kerr is Australia's all-time leading scorer, for both men and women. ⚽

Position: Forward ⚽
Country: Australia 🇦🇺

Sam Kerr grew up in **Australia** with a soccer ball at her feet and a fearless spirit. From kicking around in her backyard in Perth to lighting up stadiums across the world, Sam has become one of the greatest goal scorers the game has ever seen.

Sam *dominated* the soccer field. In both the **NWSL** and the **W-League**, Sam smashed goal-scoring records and left defenders wondering how she always seemed one step ahead. Her timing, movement, and finishing skills make her a nightmare to defend and a thrill to watch. Whether she's scoring a header or racing past the back line, Sam knows how to put the ball in the net and she makes it look effortless.

What sets Sam apart is how she always seems to be in the right place at the right time. Her goals aren't just luck. They're the result of quick thinking, sharp instincts, and a relentless desire to be the decisive factor for her team. Even when the pressure is high, Sam exemplifies a forward's leadership by consistently making game-changing runs and delivering clutch finishes, like her unforgettable **2023 World Cup** goal against **England**. She blasted a goal from outside the box that had the whole world cheering. Even when the pressure is highest, Sam steps up and delivers.

But Sam's story isn't only about scoring goals. She's become a *role model* for kids everywhere. Thanks to her, more girls in Australia and around the world see soccer as something they can do and excel at. Sam has helped raise the profile of women's soccer and made it exciting to dream big on the pitch.

Off the field, Sam uses her voice to make a difference. She has spoken up for more support for women athletes and has joined programs that provide kids with better access to sports. Whether she's visiting schools or helping run soccer clinics, she believes in lifting others up and giving back to the game that gave her so much.

Sam demonstrates that greatness stems from passion, consistent effort, and self-belief. Her talent is impressive, but it's her mindset that keeps her going, especially when things get tough.

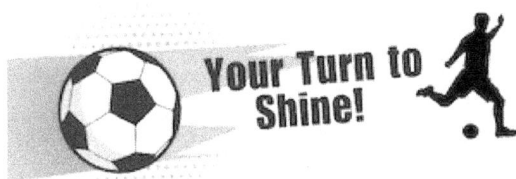

Kick It Like Sam!

Want to score goals like Sam Kerr? Try this fun mini challenge:

1. **Think like a striker.** Set up cones or shoes in your yard or park and practice finding open space, just like Sam does.

2. **Perfect your shot.** Take five shots with your dominant foot, then five with your other. Which one needs more practice?

3. **Celebrate your way.** Create your own signature goal celebration. A dance? A cartwheel? A silly face? You choose!

Write or draw your **best goal moment** in the journal below. What did it feel like to score?

NOTES

GOAL CELEBRATION:

- [ ] ....
- [ ] ....
- [ ] ....
- [ ] ....

Write or draw your best goal moment.

As we finish this chapter on today's soccer legends, take a moment to think about what makes each one stand out. Messi *plays with heart*, Ronaldo *never stops pushing himself*, Mbappé brings *speed* and *creativity*, Morgan *leads with strength and spirit*, and Kerr knows how to *light up a game* with every goal. These stars prove that soccer sparks big dreams.

So the next time you kick a ball, cheer from the stands, or watch a match at home, think about what you can learn from their stories. With effort, passion, and a little bit of courage, you can chase big goals too.

Up next: meet the rising stars who are already making their mark and showing the world what the future of soccer looks like!

CHAPTER 4: RISING STARS TO WATCH

Trinity Rodman

Alphonso Davies

Jadon Sancho

Salma Paralluelo

Jude Bellingham

The message to the young players is that hard work and dedication are everything. As a footballer or anything in life, if you're dedicated, you have to fight for that and don't give up, however hard it is.

— Alphonso Davies

What does it take to shine on the world stage before you're even old enough to rent a car? In this chapter, we meet the rising stars who prove that age is just a number when you've got *passion, persistence,* and *a love for the game* that can't be taught.

We'll kick off with **Jude Bellingham**, whose fearless rise turned heads in top leagues. You'll discover how **Alphonso** Davies sprinted past every obstacle, from a refugee camp to the world's biggest stadiums. Then there's **Jadon Sancho**, whose creative footwork and playful flair turned matches into highlights. **Trinity Rodman** shows what happens when you combine raw talent with unstoppable drive, while **Salma Paralluelo** lights up the field with speed, spark, and a champion's heart.

These young stars aren't just great because they score goals or make clever passes. They're great because they remind us that dreams don't have to wait. Every kick, every sprint, and every setback they overcome shows that courage starts now, no matter your age. So, get your cleats on and get ready to be inspired! These new heroes are already changing the game, and their stories are sure to light a fire in you.

4.1 From Boots to Brilliance: Jude Bellingham's Rise

The Midfield Maestro

JUDE BELLINGHAM

Midfielder   England   2023 Golden Boy Award

In Birmingham, **England**, a young boy named **Jude Bellingham** spent his early days kicking a soccer ball around with friends. Even as a little kid, he was all in: fast feet, quick thinking, and a love for the game that seemed to grow with every touch of the ball. At just *eight years old*, Jude joined **Birmingham City**'s academy. Coaches immediately noticed that he had something special.

The Prodigy Takes Flight

By *sixteen*, Jude was already making club history. He became the youngest player ever to appear for *Birmingham City's first team*. Walking onto the field as a teenager during a professional match takes serious courage, the kind of pressure that would rattle most adults. But Jude didn't just handle it. He thrived.

What makes Jude stand out is his exceptional understanding of the game. He can play different roles in midfield, switching positions and adjusting to the team's needs like a seasoned professional. His decisions are lightning-fast and intelligent. He always seems to know where to pass, when to tackle, and how to move into space. That versatility caught the attention of top European clubs.

Global Stage, Golden Touch

Jude signed with **Borussia Dortmund** in **Germany**, where he honed his skills against some of the world's best players. This was a pivotal moment, a significant leap out of his comfort zone. As Jude himself put it, "*I just want to be Jude and go on my own path*." He sought challenges and growth, and Dortmund offered that opportunity. Then came a massive step: a transfer to **Real Madrid**, one of the most legendary clubs in soccer history. Big stadiums, tough matches, global fans. Jude rose to the challenge, scoring crucial goals and quickly becoming a fan favorite.

By *seventeen*, he had earned his first cap for the English national team. When most players his age were just getting into high school teams, Jude was competing on the international stage. He proved he belonged, not by playing it safe but by making bold, game-changing moves. During major tournaments, he didn't just show up. He stood out.

People love to compare Jude to past legends like **Steven Gerrard** or **Frank Lampard**. But Jude isn't trying to copy anyone. He's carving out his own path and inspiring others along the way.

Your Soccer Dream

If you could fast-forward a few years, where would you be in the soccer world? Scoring a winning goal in a championship match? Leading your team as captain? Or maybe passing the ball that sets up the game-winning play?

Take a moment to dream big, then write or draw your vision below.

1. **Pick your dream position**: striker, defender, midfielder, or goalkeeper.

2. **Invent your own team name and colors.**

3. **Imagine your first big match**: who are you playing against, and what's the final score?

Jude's journey shows what can happen when you stay focused and trust your love for the game. From his relentless practicing with friends in Birmingham to making history as Birmingham City's youngest player, his dedication to mastering different midfield roles proves that **consistent effort, one step at a time, makes all the difference.**

4.2 Strong Steps: How Alphonso Davies Beat the Odds

The Roadrunner

ALPHONSO DAVIES

Left Back/ Winger

Canada

First Canadian to win UEFA Champions League

Before **Alphonso Davies** became one of the fastest players in the world, he was a kid facing challenges most of us can only imagine. He was born in a *refugee camp* in **Ghana**, where soccer balls were rare and fields were nothing more than patches of dirt. His parents had fled **Liberia's civil war**, searching for a safer place to raise their family.

When Alphonso was *five*, his family moved to **Canada**. Life in Edmonton was full of firsts: first snowfall, first school day, and his first real chance to play soccer. He joined a free after-school league called Free Footie, where kids could play without needing to buy uniforms or equipment. Right away, coaches noticed Alphonso's raw talent and his unstoppable energy. He ran faster, worked harder, and smiled wider than almost anyone else on the field.

Alphonso's *speed* is now legendary. Watching him race down the field feels like watching someone hit fast-forward. He flies past defenders, charges up the wing, and makes plays that leave fans shaking their heads in amazement. But he's more than just fast. He can defend, pass, and score. He tackles with precision, times his runs perfectly, and isn't afraid to take chances. Whether he's stopping a goal or setting one up, Alphonso plays with wholehearted focus every single minute.

At **Bayern Munich**, one of Europe's biggest clubs, Alphonso quickly became a starter and helped the team win the **UEFA Champions League**. His fearless style of play earned respect from teammates and opponents alike. And when he pulls on Canada's national team jersey, he plays with immense pride, giving everything to lift his team and his country.

Off the pitch, Alphonso uses his platform to inspire. He became an ambassador for the **United Nations High Commissioner for Refugees (UNHCR)**, speaking out for people who've had to flee their homes, just like his own family once did.

"I want kids everywhere to know that your beginning doesn't define your future." *he often says. "Dreams can grow in even the hardest places."*

He also stands up for *fairness in sports*. He openly discusses *diversity* and the importance of giving everyone a chance, regardless of their background. To Alphonso, the game should be open to everyone who loves it.

Alphonso Davies's story is one of grit, heart, and hope. From a dusty refugee camp to cheering crowds in packed stadiums, his relentless energy on the field, honed from early days in a free after-school league, proves that even the toughest beginnings can lead to powerful futures when you chase your dreams with everything you've got.

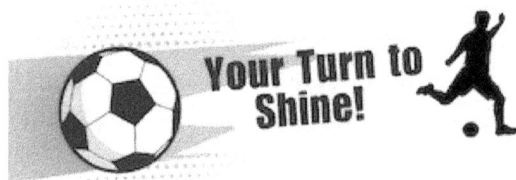

Your Turn to Shine!

Run like Alphonso!

Think you've got speed? Time to put it to the test!

1. **Set up a short race** in a safe space, your backyard, school field, or even a hallway.

2. **Have someone time you** running twenty meters (about half a basketball court).

3. **Try to beat your time** in three runs. What helped you go faster?

Challenge: Alphonso can run **35 km/h** during a game. That's as fast as a roller coaster just starting to zoom! How close can you get?

4.3 Flair on the Field: Meet Jadon Sancho

The Street Artist

JADON SANCHO

Midfielder   England   Dazzling Dribbles
and Creativity

Jadon Sancho grew up in Kennington, **London**, where football (as it's called in England) wasn't just a game. It was a way of life. If you passed by the parks or schoolyards in his neighbourhood, chances are you'd see Jadon dribbling down the pavement. He played every chance he got, turning sidewalks into training grounds and daydreams into goals. From the very beginning, it was clear: Jadon didn't just love football. He lived it.

The Audacious Leap

As Jadon got older, his talent grew too big to stay local. He trained at the **Manchester City** academy, one of the top youth programs in England. But he wanted more than the bench. He wanted to play, to learn, to create on the field. So, at just *seventeen*, he made a bold move: He left England for Germany to join **Borussia Dortmund**. Some people doubted his decision. Why leave a famous club for something uncertain? But Jadon wasn't chasing comfort. He was chasing *growth*.

That leap of faith changed everything.

Artistry and Advocacy

At Dortmund, Jadon found his rhythm, and the world took notice. He played with style, swagger, and unbelievable skill. His footwork dazzled, his passes sliced through defenses, and his creativity made every match exciting to watch. Defenders couldn't keep up. Fans couldn't get enough. Whether he was scoring goals or setting them up, Jadon made the game look like art in motion.

What made his story even more powerful was how it inspired other young players. Jadon showed *that stepping outside your comfort zone* could open massive doors. Suddenly, more English players were heading to European clubs, following his lead. He helped change the game, not just with his feet but with his fearlessness.

Off the pitch, Jadon proved he's just as brave. He's used his voice to stand up for what's right, especially against *racism* and *injustice*. After scoring a goal in **2020**, he lifted his jersey to reveal a message: *Justice for George Floyd*. That moment echoed around the world, reminding fans that athletes can lead with both skill and heart.

Jadon Sancho's journey isn't just about fancy footwork or highlight reels. It's about *daring to be different,* a leap of faith seen when he left a top

English academy at seventeen for Borussia Dortmund to find consistent playing time. His story proves that real greatness comes from staying true to yourself and using your talents to make a difference for others

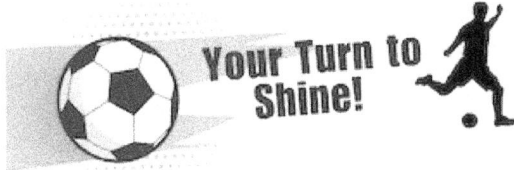

Create like Sancho

Jadon plays with creativity, and you can too!

Try this fun activity:

1. **Pick your three favorite moves:** a pass, a dribble, and a celebration.

2. **Give your combo a name** (like The Sancho Shuffle or Lightning Pass).

3. **Practice it until it feels uniquely yours,** then show it off at your next game or playtime.

Bonus: Draw yourself in action wearing your dream team jersey. What colors would you wear? What number is on your back?

4.4 Trinity Rodman's Power: Speed, Strength, and Spirit

The Spark

TRINITY RODMAN

Forward   United States   Youngest Player
                                                    Drafted to NWSL

Trinity Rodman's rise to soccer fame is as thrilling as a last-minute goal in a championship game. Her dad, **Dennis Rodman,** was a famous basketball player, but Trinity wanted to shine in her own way. While others expected her to grab a basketball, Trinity chose the soccer field instead. From a young age, she was more interested in chasing down balls than shooting hoops. This was her "Aha!" moment, the realization that her passion lay squarely on the pitch.

She loved the game so much that she skipped college to pursue a professional career in it. That decision made her the *youngest* player ever drafted in the **National Women's Soccer League**. Talk about making a bold move!

Trinity's playing style is fierce and fearless. She charges down the field with fire in her eyes, always looking for the goal. Her speed, strength, and confidence are helping to reshape how people see women's soccer. Every time she scores, she shows young athletes everywhere that anything is possible when you *believe* in yourself.

But Trinity's path wasn't easy. Being the daughter of a celebrity meant people expected a lot. It felt like the spotlight followed her everywhere, even before she proved herself on the field. Instead of letting the pressure break her, Trinity used it as fuel. She trained harder, focused deeper, and pushed herself to be the best version of herself.

Her dedication is paying off tremendously. More girls are picking up soccer balls and dreaming of big games because of what Trinity's shown them. She's not just scoring goals, she's also opening doors for the next generation.

Trinity Rodman reminds us that you don't have to copy anyone's story. Despite the pressures of a famous parent, she forged her own path by dedicating herself to soccer, proving that with fierce grit and focused training, you can go from dreamer to *game changer.*

Your Turn to Shine!

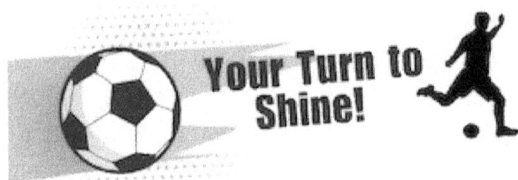

Be Your Own Star

What makes you different? What do you love that feels totally you, even if it's not what people expect?

Try this:

1. Write down one big goal you have.

2. Now, list three things you'll do this week to take a small step toward it.

Bonus: Draw yourself achieving that goal, jersey, pose, and all!

4.5 Salma Paralluelo's Spark: Born to Be a Champion

The Dual Talent

SALMA PARALLUELO

Forward

Spain

Salma was once a professional sprinter

Before she lit up soccer stadiums, **Salma Paralluelo** was sprinting down tracks like lightning. She was one of **Spain**'s top young sprinters, known for her speed and heart-pounding finishes. But Salma had more than one dream.

Salma wasn't content with being great at just one sport. While dominating on the *track*, she was also making defenders sweat on the *soccer* field. For a while, she balanced both worlds, training for championships and playing soccer at a high level. Few athletes could maintain that kind of pace.

Then came her boldest move yet: Salma chose to put her full focus on soccer, joining none other than **FC Barcelona**, one of the world's best women's teams.

From the moment she stepped onto the pitch, her impact was electric. Blazing speed, silky footwork, and a fierce left foot turned matches on their heads. Watching her on the wing feels like watching wind itself: quick, unstoppable, and thrilling.

In the **2023 Women's World Cup**, Salma helped lead **Spain** to their *first-ever title*. She scored crucial goals, made game-changing plays, and became a national hero. But Salma's impact doesn't stop at the final whistle.

She's also a proud role model. With roots in **Equatorial Guinea** on her mother's side, she inspires girls across **Spain, Africa,** and beyond. She shows that you don't have to fit into one box. You can chase all your passions and still succeed.

Not many athletes would walk away from being a top sprinter to start over in soccer. But Salma trusted her instincts, worked harder than ever, and became a **World Cup champion**.

Mix Your Passions

Salma followed her heart across **two sports** before finding her moment in the spotlight. What do you love to do?

Try this:

1. Pick two things you enjoy, maybe it's soccer and painting, or science and skateboarding.

2. How could you mix them into something amazing?

3. Draw or describe your own "power combo" talent!

Young stars like Trinity and Salma are proving something powerful: you don't have to wait to make an impact. **You don't have to choose between dreams**. And **you definitely don't need to follow anyone else's path**.

Whether you're sprinting toward a goal, standing up for what's right, or daring to be different, your story matters. Keep going. You might just be the next star someone else looks up to.

You've seen how determination can turn dreams into reality. Now get ready to meet the amazing women who didn't just chase their soccer dreams, they broke down walls and opened doors for every girl who came after them.

CHAPTER 5: THE WOMEN WHO CHANGED THE GAME

My coach said I ran like a girl. I said if he tried a little harder, he could too.

— Mia Hamm

Who says soccer is just for boys? Around the world, women who led the way have laced up their boots, stepped onto the pitch, and proved that passion, skill, and courage have no gender. This chapter is all about them: the fearless girls and women who turned dreams into history and showed millions that it's okay to take up space, speak up, and play hard.

We'll start with **Marta Vieira da Silva**, whose dazzling dribbles and record-breaking goals earned her a crown in the hearts of fans everywhere. Then meet **Ada Hegerberg**, who used her talent and her voice to stand up for fairness in the sport she loves. Travel alongside **Asisat Oshoala**, who chased big dreams from Nigeria all the way to the top leagues. And finally, discover how **Megan Rapinoe** pairs fierce play with fearless words, reminding everyone that sport can change hearts and minds.

These stories prove soccer isn't just about winning games. It's about winning respect, lifting others, and daring to be different. Whether you're a girl who loves the game or someone cheering from the sidelines, these heroes show that strength comes in many forms, and it often starts with simply saying, "*Why not me?*"

5.1 Crowned in Cleats: Marta's Soccer Journey

MARTA DA SILVA
The Queen of Football

MIDFIELDER
BRAZIL

FIFA WOMEN'S WORLD PLAYER

Marta is the first woman to win 6 FIFA Women's World Player of the Year awards

In the small town of Dois Riachos, **Brazil**, a barefoot girl chased a soccer ball through the dusty streets. That girl was **Marta Vieira da Silva**, who would one day be known around the world as the *Queen of Soccer*. She didn't have fancy cleats or a shiny field. She played with anything she could find, turning sticks into goalposts and sidewalks into stadiums. What she had was *skill, grit,* and a *heart* that beat for the game.

From Humble Pitches to Professional Stages

Marta's raw talent was impossible to ignore. She joined local teams, trained with boys, and never backed down from a challenge. Scouts took notice early. They saw something rare, *speed, precision,* and a fierce *love* for the sport. Soon, Marta headed to **Sweden** to play professionally. Leaving home wasn't easy, but she was ready. She dazzled fans with her footwork and her flair. Watching her dribble was like watching magic. The defenders didn't stand a chance.

Back home in Brazil, where soccer is like oxygen, Marta became a superstar. Girls who once felt invisible on the pitch now saw someone like them leading the way. She wasn't just winning games, she was *changing* the game.

A Queen with a Cause

But Marta didn't stop at goals and trophies. She raised her voice for equal treatment in sports. She spoke out against unfair pay and advocated for girls who wanted to be taken seriously. At the World Cup, after a tough loss, Marta gave a powerful speech that made headlines. She told the world:

It's time to believe in women's soccer and time for the next generation to step up.

Marta's trophy shelf is packed with *six* **FIFA World Player of the Year** awards. She's Brazil's all-time leading goal scorer, yes, even *more than* Pelé. But her biggest victory might be the girls she's inspired. Today, thousands of kids lace up their cleats because they saw Marta do it first. Her journey proves that greatness doesn't depend on where you start. It depends on how hard you play and how boldly you dream.

Marta didn't just become a soccer legend, she became a *force for change*. It's about fighting for fairness, making space for others, and her unwavering *pursuit of excellence*, honed from barefoot games in dusty streets.

Every time she steps on the field, her unparalleled skill and courageous voice for equal treatment remind the world that passion, courage, and talent can change everything.

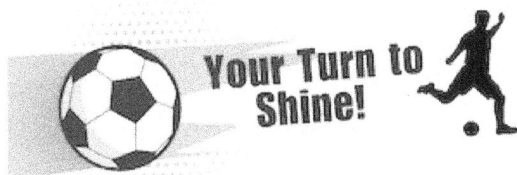

Your Turn to Shine!

What Would You Change?

Marta spoke up to help make sports better for girls everywhere. What would you change to make sports more fair or fun for everyone?

Try this:

1. Write down one thing you'd change in sports (rules, uniforms, teams, anything).

2. Now write how that change would help people play better, feel stronger, or be more included.

3. Share your idea with a friend or coach and see what they think!

Even small ideas can lead to big change. You never know who you might inspire.

5.2 Ada's Voice, Ada's Victory

ADA HEGERBERG

The Goal Machine

FORWARD
NORWAY

BALLON D'OR FÉMININ

Ada is the first woman to win the Ballon d'Or Féminin in 2018.

It's impossible to play football in a world among men and not fight for equality.

— Ada Hegerberg

Some players are known for their goals. **Ada Hegerberg**? She's known for those and for shaking up the system.

Rising Star, Brewing Discontent

Before she was making history in France, Ada was just a kid in **Norway** with a serious love for the game. She and her sister trained like pros, practicing moves and building the kind of grit that doesn't show up on a stat sheet. By the time she hit the European leagues, Ada wasn't there to participate. She was there to *compete*. At **Olympique Lyonnais**, she became a scoring machine, helping her team dominate the **UEFA Women's Champions League** and smashing records along the way. But numbers only tell part of her story.

The Bold Stand for Equality

In **2017**, Ada made a decision that stunned the sports world: She stepped away from Norway's national team. Why? She believed female players weren't being treated fairly and wanted action, not just promises. It was bold. It was risky. And it sent a message louder than any goal celebration: *respect us, or we won't play*.

Ada didn't fade into the background. She became the first-ever woman to win the **Ballon d'Or Féminin**, and when she stepped up to accept it, she didn't just thank her teammates, she challenged the whole world to do better. Her voice carried far beyond the stadium, rallying fans, players, and leaders to rethink how women in sports are valued.

Her stand sparked real change. More conversations. More support. More eyes on the women's game. And in Norway, policies began to shift, a proof that courage can move the needle.

Your Turn to Shine!

What Matters to You?

If something feels unfair, what's one way you could speak up?

1. Think of something you'd like to change at school, at practice, or in your community.

2. What's a small but powerful step you could take?

3. Write a short message or draw a sign that shares your idea. You might be surprised who listens!

You don't need a trophy to be brave. Just heart, like Ada, whose bold decision to step away from the national team over unfair treatment spoke louder than any goal, ultimately sparking real change for women in sports.

5.3 Big Dreams, Far Travels: Meet Asisat Oshoala

Asisat is a six-time African Women's Player of the Year — the most in history.

One hot afternoon in Lagos, **Nigeria**, a barefoot girl weaved through a crowd of boys during a street match, dribbling, sprinting, and scoring like she had rockets in her shoes. That girl was **Asisat Oshoala**. Long before she became one of the world's most feared strikers, she was lighting up local fields with her speed and fire. Her neighborhood might not have had fancy turf or shiny equipment, but it had something better: *pure love for the game*. Every match was a chance to prove herself. And she did, again and again.

The Journey Begins in Lagos

Asisat faced the unique challenge of being a girl in a sport often dominated by boys in her community. But her talent was undeniable. She usually describes her early days with a fierce determination:

"I just wanted to play. The field was my escape, my happy place. I didn't care who I was playing against, only that I was playing."

This raw passion propelled her forward, even when resources were scarce. Her big leap came when she moved to Europe, playing for top teams across the continent and eventually landing at **FC Barcelona**.

Conquering Europe and Giving Back

At Barcelona, she became a key player in the club's rise to dominance in the **UEFA Women's Champions League**. Her goals were electric, her movements unpredictable. Oshoala didn't just show up, she took over. In 2021, she made history as the *first African woman* to play for and help lead **Barcelona** to a **Champions League title**, a monumental achievement that shattered barriers. Her style? Explosive. She bursts forward like a sprinter, outpacing defenders with ease. Her footwork is sharp, her instincts razor-fast. In high-stakes moments, when tension fills the stadium, Oshoala often delivers the game-winning goal: cool, calm, and clutch. Fans across Africa and Europe watch her in awe, knowing something special is about to happen whenever she touches the ball.

But what sets her apart isn't just what she does during the game. It's what she's building beyond it. Through the **Asisat Oshoala Foundation**, she's giving girls in **Nigeria** the chance to chase their dreams, just like she did. From soccer clinics to scholarships, she's creating real opportunities for girls who might not otherwise get them. Her goal? To make sure talent doesn't get left behind just because of where someone grows up.

Oshoala proves that greatness can start anywhere, even in the dusty corners of a crowded neighbourhood. Her story is a powerful reminder: *it's not where you start, but how far you're willing to go*, as demonstrated by her relentless training that propelled her from Lagos Street matches to becoming FC Barcelona's key striker. With grit, generosity, and a whole lot of hustle, she's going all the way, also building opportunities for other girls through her foundation.

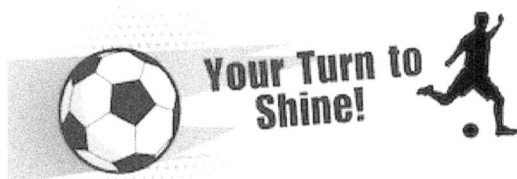

Dream Big!

What's your biggest dream? Maybe it's becoming a soccer star, writing a book, or building something amazing. Whatever it is, don't just think it; start chasing it!

Grab a piece of paper and do one of these:
1. Write it down in big, bold letters: *"One day, I will..."*

2. Draw a picture of you reaching your dream, scoring the winning goal, standing on stage, or holding your trophy.

3. Then, hide it somewhere special, under your pillow, inside your backpack, or in a favorite book.

Whenever you feel tired or frustrated, take a peek at it. Let it remind you that every big dream begins with one small step. **Your dream isn't too far. It's just waiting for you to go after it.**

5.4 From Seoul to the World: Ji So-yun's Soccer Adventure

JI SO-YUN

The Korean Playmaker

⚽ MIDFIELDER
SOUTH KOREA

Ji So-Yun is South Korea's all-time top scorer (men or women), with over 70 international goals.

In a small town in South Korea, **Ji So-yun** grew up chasing a soccer ball through narrow streets and neighbourhood parks. She played with *determination* that stood out, even when she was the only girl on the field. Her feet moved fast, her mind even quicker. Coaches saw more than just a talented player. They saw a spark.

That spark carried her to **Japan**, where she joined **INAC Kobe Leonessa** as a teenager. She didn't just keep up; she dominated. Ji played with elegance and precision, quickly rising to become one of the league's brightest stars. But she wasn't done. She faced the challenge of adapting to new cultures and languages, but her resolve was stronger than any barrier.

Ji took another bold step and moved to England to join **Chelsea FC**. Competing in the **FA Women's Super League**, she brought a new style of play that combined speed, skill, and brilliant vision. In a league packed with talent, Ji held her own and then some. Emma Hayes, her coach at Chelsea, often lauded her, saying:

" Ji is a genius. She sees things nobody else sees. She can unlock any defence."

Her magic lies in the way she reads the game. As a midfielder, Ji doesn't just pass the ball, she creates moments. One second, she's collecting the ball from the back, the next she's slicing through defences with a pass no one saw coming. She can switch directions, surprise opponents, and turn tight spaces into goal-scoring chances. And yes, she scores too, often with stunning shots that curl past keepers and send fans into cheers.

Back home, Ji became a national hero. She's **South Korea's** *all-time leading goal scorer* and one of the most respected athletes in the country. But her story means more than goals and trophies. Ji's journey shattered stereotypes and showed young girls in Asia that soccer isn't just for boys. It's for anyone with the *courage to chase a dream.*

Ji has faced plenty of challenges, language barriers, homesickness, and adjusting to new cultures. But she met each one with quiet strength. Her success across three countries proves that greatness doesn't depend on where you're from. It grows from what's inside you.

Ji So-yun doesn't just play the game; she also connects worlds through it. She's a quiet force who has changed the face of women's soccer in Asia and beyond, showcasing how her diligent practice and brilliant vision as a midfielder have allowed her to dominate in Japan and England. Through her journey, she reminds young athletes everywhere that big dreams can cross oceans when fueled by consistent *dedication* and *perseverance*.

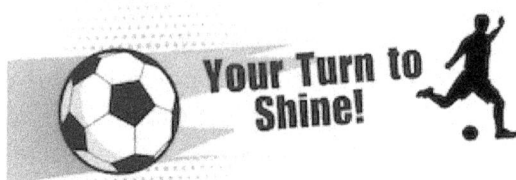
Your Turn to Shine!

Across the Field and Around the World

Ji So-yun moved across countries and cultures to follow her dream. She didn't let new languages, unfamiliar places, or being far from home stop her from playing the game she loves. Now it's your turn to imagine your own global soccer adventure!

Activity: Build Your Dream Team from Around the World

1. **Choose 5 countries** you'd love to visit or play soccer in.

2. For each country, **pick a teammate**. It can be a made-up name, a real player you admire, or even a character you invent.

3. **Give each teammate strength**. Are they super fast? Do they make excellent passes? Are they fearless goalies?

4. **Draw your team's jersey** and write your team's name on the provided sheet.

Then answer this: **How would you help your team work together**, even if everyone speaks different languages or comes from other cultures? **Write 2–3 sentences about what you would do to bring the team together**, just like Ji did.

Build Your Dream Team
Around the World

COUNTRY 1	NAME OF COUNTRY: TEAMATE: STRENGTH(S):	**Team Name & Jersey**
COUNTRY 2	NAME OF COUNTRY: TEAMATE: STRENGTH(S):	
COUNTRY 3	NAME OF COUNTRY: TEAMATE: STRENGTH(S):	
COUNTRY 4	NAME OF COUNTRY: TEAMATE: STRENGTH(S):	**How You Can Help:**
COUNTRY 5	NAME OF COUNTRY: TEAMATE: STRENGTH(S):	

5.5 Megan's Message: Play Hard, Speak Loud

MEGAN RAPINOE

Pinoe

⚽ WINGER / FORWARD
🇺🇸 UNITED STATES

USA
15

Megan is the winner of the 2019 Ballon d'Or Féminin and Golden Boot at the FIFA Women's World Cup. 🏆 🌐

The more I've been able to learn about gay rights and equal pay and gender equity and racial inequality, the more that it all intersects. You can't really pick it apart. It's all intertwined.

—Megan Rapinoe

When you think of a soccer hero, **Megan Rapinoe** might just be the first name that pops into your head. She's not only a superstar on the field but also a powerful voice off it. With the **US Women's National Team**, she's achieved incredible success, winning World Cups and Olympic gold medals. Her *skills* and *leadership* have helped her team shine brightly on the world stage. But Megan's impact goes beyond soccer. She's a bold advocate for social justice, speaking up for equality and fairness. She doesn't just play soccer; she plays for change.

Megan's bravery in standing up for what she believes in is truly inspiring. Imagine having the courage to kneel during the national anthem to show support for others. That's exactly what Megan did, standing in solidarity with those fighting for justice. Despite facing criticism and backlash, she continued to push for equal pay and visibility in women's sports. She knew that change was necessary, and she wasn't afraid to speak out to make it happen. Her determination showed everyone that standing up for what's right is always worth it.

Inclusivity is at the heart of what Megan stands for. She champions *diversity* in both sport and society. She campaigns tirelessly for LGBTQ+ rights, ensuring everyone feels welcome and accepted. Megan believes that sports should be accessible to everyone, regardless of who you are or where you come from. She uses her voice to speak up for those who might not have one and fights for underrepresented voices in athletics. Her work makes sports more inclusive, opening doors for everyone to participate.

Young athletes look up to Megan Rapinoe not just for her soccer skills but for her *courage* and *authenticity*. She promotes *self-expression*, encouraging kids to be themselves and share their unique talents with the world. Megan actively mentors young female players, inspiring them to *dream big* and *strive for excellence*. Her influence extends far beyond the soccer field, demonstrating to the next generation that by consistently playing hard and speaking out for justice, they too can make a difference in the world.

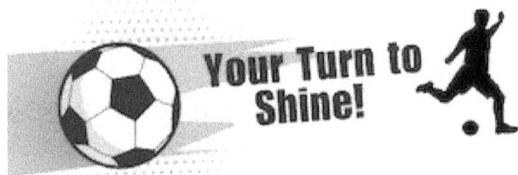

Your Turn to Shine!

Speak up like Megan

Megan Rapinoe used her voice to stand up for justice, fairness, and equality, even when it wasn't easy. Now it's your turn to think about what you believe in and how you can make a difference!

1. What matters to you?
Think about something in your world you wish could change. It could be something big, like helping the planet, or something small, like making sure everyone gets a turn at recess.
Write down your answer: *"I want to speak up for…"* Or draw a picture of what you care about.

2. Make a mini poster.
On a blank sheet of paper, create a mini-poster with your message. Add bold words, pictures, or symbols to show what you stand for. Example messages: *"Everyone deserves a chance to play!"*, *"Be kind. Speak up.",* *"Fair is fair!"*
You can hang your poster in your room, locker, or share it with your class or team.

3. Your brave plan.
Write or talk about one thing you can do this week to support your cause. Maybe it's including someone new at lunch, helping a team-mate, or starting a kindness chain.
"One way I'll speak up is…"

Just like Megan Rapinoe, **your voice matters**. You don't need a stadium or a gold medal to make an impact. You just need courage and a message worth sharing.

As we close this chapter, consider how some players utilize their platform to lead with heart and purpose. Their actions remind us that soccer can be more than just a game. It can spark change, bring people together, and build strong communities. These athletes demonstrate that *courage, kindness,* and *leadership* are just as important as skill.

Next, we'll explore how soccer helps shape life skills that extend far beyond the field. From handling pressure to working as a team, the lessons you learn in the game can help you grow in every part of your life.

Make Your Best Pass Yet

You've kicked off an incredible journey through *Epic Soccer Stories* — and now it's your chance to make the winning play!

By leaving a review, you'll help other young readers discover these powerful stories of grit, teamwork, and game-changing heroes. Just like a perfect assist leads to a game-winning goal, your words can inspire someone else to fall in love with the beautiful game.

Why Your Review Matters

Every review is a back-of-the-net moment:
• It helps new readers find the book
• It spreads the magic of soccer across the world
• It inspires kids to dream big and play bold

Scan the QR code or click below to leave your review on Amazon:
https://www.amazon.com/review/review-your-purchases/?asin=B0FTYBD8TZ

Thank you for being part of the *Epic Soccer Stories* team.
Your review is a goal that keeps the passion for soccer alive and kicking!

Let's score one for the team!
—Dylan Ambrose
Epic Sports for Kids | YearnMoreBooks.com

CHAPTER 6: MORE THAN A GAME: LIFE LESSONS FROM THE PITCH

Playing football is very simple, but playing simple football is the hardest thing there is.

– Johan Cruyff

Soccer dazzles us with fancy footwork, big goals, and shiny trophies, but it also teaches us something deeper. It shapes how we handle pressure, work as a team, and keep going when the game feels lost. Those lessons last long after the final whistle. In this chapter, we'll explore how the game helps kids (and even grown-ups) grow stronger inside and out.

We'll see how bouncing back after a missed shot or tough loss builds *resilience*, and why learning to pass, listen, and trust teammates creates real unity. You'll discover that true sportsmanship isn't just shaking hands after a game, it's treating everyone with respect, win or lose. There's also *confidence* and *discipline*: showing up to practice, giving your best, and believing in yourself even when it feels hard. And, of course, there's the idea of never giving up: always chasing that next goal, on or off the field.

Finally, we'll talk about *friendship* and *rivalry*, how healthy competition can push you to grow and how teammates can become lifelong friends. Soccer teaches that the real victories often aren't written on a scoreboard but in the person you become while playing.

So lace up and step onto this next page because these life skills might just help you score big wherever your journey leads!

6.1 When You Lose, Learn

You're racing down the field. The crowd's buzzing. Then bam! You miss the shot. That sinking feeling? Every player knows it. But great athletes don't stop there, they learn, adjust, and come back stronger.

Marcus Rashford knows that feeling all too well. Imagine you're one of England's biggest soccer stars, playing for **Manchester United**, when suddenly your body betrays you. Rashford suffered a serious back injury that kept him off the field for months. *"Will I ever play the same way again?"* he wondered during those dark days of recovery. While his teammates trained and played, Marcus spent countless hours in physical therapy, slowly rebuilding his strength. Some days, even walking hurts. But instead of feeling sorry for himself, Rashford used that time to study the game even deeper. He watched endless hours of film, analyzed his technique, and came back not just physically healed, but smarter and mentally tougher than ever. When he finally returned to the pitch, fans could see the difference. He wasn't just the same old Rashford; he was a *warrior* who had conquered his biggest fear.

Then there's **Linda Caicedo** from **Colombia**, whose story will absolutely blow your mind. At a young age of *fourteen*, she was already good enough to turn professional! She was living every young player's dream, racing down soccer fields with her lightning speed and dazzling footwork. But then came news that would terrify anyone: doctors found ovarian cancer. At just fifteen, Linda faced surgeries, treatments, and the very real possibility that her soccer career might be over before it really began. "*Why me? Why now?*" she must have wondered.

But here's what makes Linda extraordinary: while other kids her age worried about homework and friend drama, she was fighting for her life and winning. During treatment, when she was too weak to train, she'd watch soccer videos and visualize herself playing again. "*I'll be back*," she told herself every single day. And guess what? She kept that promise. Today, Linda doesn't just play soccer; she flies across the field for **Real Madrid** and represents **Colombia** in the **World Cup**, her smile as bright as her blazing speed. Every goal she scores tells the same amazing story: *dreams don't die*, they just wait for you to get back up and chase them again.

This kind of resilience isn't just about physical strength, it's about mental toughness. Both Marcus and Linda learned that setbacks don't define you; how you respond to them does. They turned their biggest challenges into their greatest comebacks.

These skills don't just help on the soccer field. They work in school and life too. Got a tough grade? Use it as motivation to study harder and try again.

Your Turn to Shine!

Bounce Back Challenge!

Think about a time something didn't go your way, maybe at school, during a game, or with a friend.

1. Draw or write about what happened.

2. What did you learn from it?

3. Write one word describing how you felt when you didn't give up.

Stick that word somewhere you'll see it often. Let it remind you: **mistakes don't define you, but how you respond does.**

6.2 Winning Together

At the heart of every great soccer team is something you can't measure with stats, *trust*. No matter how skilled a player is, no one wins matches alone. Success comes from working together, sharing the ball, and supporting one another.

Look at the US Women's National Team during their championship runs. Stars like **Megan Rapinoe** and **Rose Lavelle** made headlines, but they never acted like it was a one-woman show. The team's real strength came from how tightly they played together, communicating, covering, and celebrating as one.

A perfect example? The **2017 Champions League** clash between **Barcelona** and **Paris Saint-Germain**. Barcelona had lost the first leg 4–0. Everyone thought it was over. But in the second leg, the whole team rose together, scoring six goals to complete one of the greatest comebacks in history. That win wasn't because of one superstar. It happened because *everyone* believed, passed smartly, stayed in sync, and refused to give up.

Teamwork doesn't always mean agreeing on everything. It means learning to trust each other's strengths, communicate clearly, and bounce back from mistakes together. Whether on the pitch or in real life, teamwork makes hard things easier and victories sweeter.

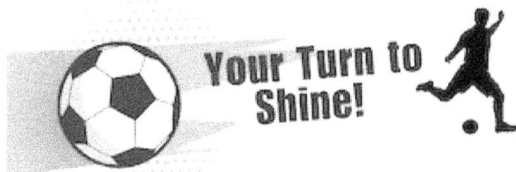
Your Turn to Shine!

Build a Team Playbook

Grab a few friends, classmates, or teammates. Together, come up with a special move or play your soccer team could try, something that uses everyone's strengths.

1. Who will start with the ball?

2. Who makes the pass?

3. Who goes for the goal?

Give your play a cool name and act it out! You can even draw it on paper like a coach designing a strategy.

Bonus challenge: Try this with a group project at school. Who's good at what? How can you work better as a team?

6.3 Playing Fair, Playing Proud

In soccer, *sportsmanship* is like the secret ingredient that makes the game more than just a match. It's all about playing fair, respecting everyone on the field, and having a good attitude, whether you win or lose. When you respect referees and your opponents, you show true sportsmanship. Winning is fantastic, but celebrating without making others feel bad is even better. It's like sharing your candy, everyone feels happier!

Let's look at some incredible stories of sportsmanship. **Paolo Di Canio**, a soccer player known for his fiery spirit, showed a different side during a **Premier League** match. The opposing goalkeeper got injured, and Paolo could have scored an easy goal. But he chose to catch the ball instead, stopping the game. This act earned him the **FIFA Fair Play Award**.

Another heartwarming example is the **Japanese team** at the **World Cup**. After their match, they cleaned up their locker room and left a thank-you note. Now that's winning hearts!

Practicing sportsmanship is fun too! Try role-playing a post-match hand-shake line with your friends. Pretend you've just finished a tough game and line up to shake hands, saying positive things like *"Great game!"* or *"Well played!"* You can also practice using positive language during games. Instead of getting upset if someone misses a goal, say, *"Nice try! Let's get it next time."* These little things make a big difference.

Sportsmanship isn't just for soccer fields. Imagine how these skills help in making friends. When you're respectful and fair, people want to hang out with you. It builds a good reputation and earns respect from others. In school or community activities, showing sportsmanship fosters teamwork and cooperation. It's like being the glue that holds everyone together.

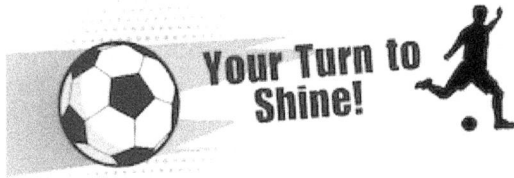

The Fair Play Challenge

Gather a few friends and create short sports skits where you act out both tricky and awesome moments on the field. You can take turns being the referee, the cheering teammate, or the player facing a challenging situation.

Here are a few scene ideas to try:

1. **A teammate misses a goal**. What do you say?

2. An opponent trips and falls. What do you do?

3. **The referee makes a call you disagree with**. How do you respond?

4. **Your team wins or loses the game**. How do you show respect?

Be creative with your scenes, add fun commentary, make crowd noises, or even use props! After each skit, talk about what kind of behaviour shows good sportsmanship and why it matters.

Why this helps: Practicing how to be fair and kind, even in high-pressure moments, builds character that lasts way beyond the soccer field. Being a good sport makes you the kind of teammate others are proud to stand beside.

6.4 Train Hard, Play Bold

You're standing in front of the goal. One shot. Everyone's watching. Your heart is racing, but your mind stays calm. That calm? That's *confidence*, the quiet belief that you're ready for the moment.

Confidence isn't something you're born with. It's built over time, especially through sports like soccer. Players train their minds just as much as their feet. They set goals, stay focused, and prepare mentally for big moments. Visualization helps. Many top athletes picture themselves scoring, passing, or staying calm before they even step onto the field. It's like creating a game plan in your head, and it works.

Discipline is what keeps that confidence steady. It's the daily decision to train, rest, eat right, and stay focused, especially when no one's watching. Take **Cristiano Ronaldo**. Beyond his flashy goals and famous name, he's known for his intense training routine and strict lifestyle. He doesn't just rely on talent; he shows up every day. That's discipline.

Lucy Bronze became one of the world's best defenders not because she was the fastest or strongest, but because she outworked everyone else. While her teammates went home after practice, Lucy stayed for extra shooting drills. When coaches said she was 'good enough,' she'd ask, '*What can I do to be better?*' Even after winning every major trophy in women's soccer, she still shows up early to training, still studies game film, still pushes herself like she's fighting for her first starting spot. That's what separates good players from legends, they never stop improving.

That's what happens when you combine natural talent with unwavering discipline, you become someone who achieves greatness and lifts others up along the way.

Discipline also shows up in small, everyday choices. Choosing to practice instead of watching TV. Getting sleep instead of scrolling late into the night. Eating foods that fuel your body, not slow it down. These little decisions create a strong foundation for confidence to grow.

And it goes beyond the field. If you're preparing for a test, performing in a play, or trying something new, confidence and discipline help you stay ready. They give you the courage to try and the habits to keep going.

Sadio Mané grew up in a tiny village called Bambali in **Senegal**, where soccer balls were made of rags and plastic bags tied together. His father, who was an imam, forbade him from playing football because he wanted Sadio to focus on his religious studies. But tragedy struck when his father died when Sadio was just seven years old. Despite this loss, Sadio kept dreaming of soccer, practicing with his homemade ball on dusty village fields. Years later, when he became a professional player earning millions, teammates were amazed by his *humility*. Instead of buying luxury cars and houses, he chose to build schools and a stadium for his village, saying:

"I do not need to display luxury cars, luxury homes, trips and even planes. I prefer that my people receive a little of what life has given me."

Even after becoming a global football star, **Sadio Mané** never forgot his roots in **Bambali**, a small village in **Senegal** with around **2,000 people**. Instead of buying Ferraris or gold watches, he used his success to **give back**.

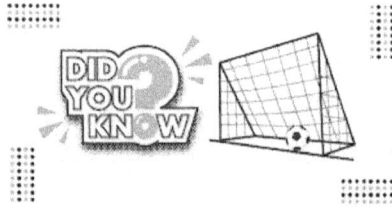

SADIO MANÉ'S AMAZING DONATIONS TO HIS VILLAGE

1 HOSPITAL
- Donated $500,000 to build a modern hospital
- Now serves 30+ villages around Bambali

2 SCHOOL
- Built a public school so kids no longer had to walk far
- Donated over $300,000 to fund education, supplies, and classrooms

3 WATER & INTERNET
- Paid for clean water wells so families don't rely on unsafe sources
- Installed free Wi-Fi so students could connect, learn, and dream big

4 COVID-19 HELP
- Donated $50,000 to Senegal's health response
- Encouraged safety and care in rural areas

5 MONTHLY SUPPORT FOR EVERY FAMILY *SUPPORT*
- Sadio gives $70 USD every month to each family in Bambali
- That helps with food, clothes, medicine, and school needs
- There are around 357 families receiving this support
- That's ~ $300,000 yearly, straight from his own earnings!

? What Does $70 Mean in Bambali?
- A full month of rice, oil, and basic food
- Notebooks and pencils for school
- Bus fare to visit the nearest city
- A lightbulb that stays on during homework time

Now **his whole village rises with him**, proof that real champions build others up.

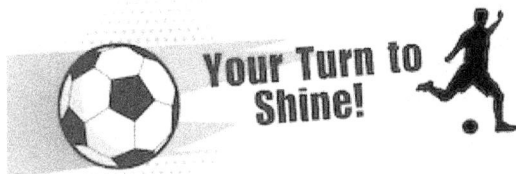

Build Your Confidence Game

Pick one thing you want to get better at, soccer, math, music, anything you love.

Now do this:

1. Write down one small goal you can reach this week.

2. Decide when and how you'll practice.

3. Close your eyes and feel what success feels like. What does it look like? How does it feel?

4. After you try it, write a sentence or draw a picture about how it went.

You don't need to be perfect. You just need to keep showing up. **Confidence grows with practice,** and you've already taken the first step.

6.5 Eyes on the Goal

Setting a big goal can feel like climbing a steep hill. It takes effort, patience, and a whole lot of heart. Some days are smooth. Others? Not so much. You might stumble or feel stuck. But every time you push forward, you're getting stronger. That's what perseverance means: sticking with something, even when it gets tough.

Just ask **Luka Modrić**.

He grew up in war-torn Croatia and was often overlooked for being too small. But he kept training, kept believing, and kept proving himself on the field. At thirty-three, an age when many midfielders begin to slow down, he led Croatia all the way to the 2018 World Cup Final and won the Ballon d'Or that same year. That wasn't luck. It was every moment he pressed on when others said he couldn't.

You don't need to be a world-famous athlete to understand that feeling. Big dreams, whether in soccer, school, music, or anything else, take time. They're built from hundreds of small steps. Setbacks will happen. But each one teaches you something and brings you closer to your goal.

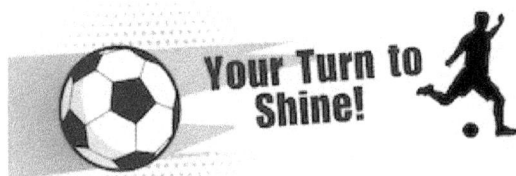
Your Turn to Shine!

Want to stay focused? Try these dream-boosting ideas:

1. **Make a dream journal.** Fill it with your goals, doodles, quotes, or anything that sparks motivation. It's like a scrapbook for your future.

2. **Create a dream board**. Use a poster or notebook page to collect images and words that represent what you're working toward. Keep it where you'll see it often.

3. **Try the Dear Future Me Challenge**. Draw your dream coming true as a comic strip. Where are you? Who's cheering? What do you say when it finally happens? Then flip to the back of your journal and write a note that begins like this:

Dear Future Me,

Remember, it wasn't just the moment you made it that mattered. It was every late night, every do-over, every time you chose to keep going instead of quitting.

I hope you still believe in those wild, wonderful dreams, because they're yours for a reason.

Keep going.

— Me (back then, dreaming big and daring to try)

Your dream is worth the work. Keep showing up. Keep believing in yourself. And when the moment comes, just like it did for Messi, you'll be ready.

LETTER TO MY
future self

Dear Me,

_____

_____

_____

_____

_____

_____

_____

_____

_____

_____

Signed:

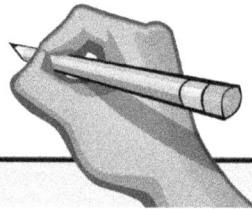

Date:

DREAM PLANNER JOURNAL

Quotes

_____
_____
_____
_____
_____

Goals for This Year

Positive Habits

_____
_____
_____
_____
_____
_____

_____
_____
_____
_____
_____
_____

Daily Motivation

_____
_____
_____

Your dream is worth the work. Keep showing up. Keep believing in yourself. And when the moment comes, just like it did for Messi, you'll be ready.

6.6 Teammates, Challengers, and Change

El Clásico

What happens when your biggest competition is also your closest friend? On the field, friendly rivalries bring out your best. You both want to win, but you're learning and growing together. Whether you're competing for a spot on the team or trying to outscore each other at practice, it keeps you sharp and can be fun too.

Take **Messi** and **Ronaldo**, for example, the greatest rivalry in soccer history! For over a decade, fans around the world would circle dates on their calendars whenever **Barcelona** played **Real Madrid**. *"El Clásico is coming!"* kids would shout at school. When these two stepped onto the same field, magic happened. Messi would dribble past five defenders like they were traffic cones, and Ronaldo would answer with a thunderous free kick that left goalkeepers speechless.

Every goal one scored seemed to inspire the other to reach new heights. Between **2008** and **2017**, these two legends completely dominated the **Ballon d'Or** for a full decade. Ronaldo struck first in 2008, then Messi answered with an incredible four straight wins (2009-2012). Not to be outdone, Ronaldo fought back with victories in 2013 and 2014, before Messi reclaimed it in 2015, and Ronaldo finished the decade strong with 2016 and 2017. For ten straight years, it was like the award had their names engraved on it before the voting even started! When one had an incredible season, the other would come back even stronger the next year. And here's an amazing fact: during their entire nine years playing in Spain together, El Clásico never ended 0-0, not once! Every match was pure fireworks. Fans would argue endlessly: *"Messi's the best!"* *"No way, Ronaldo is!"* But here's what made their rivalry truly special, they pushed each other to greatness through pure *effort, consistency,* and *pride*, never through trash talk or dirty play.

BALLON D'OR WINNERS (2005 TO 2020)

Year	Winner | Country | Club
2005	Ronaldinho |Brazil ⚽ |FC Barcelona
2006	Fabio Cannavaro | Italy ❚❚ | Real Madrid
2007	Kaká | Brazil ⚽ | AC Milan
2008	Cristiano Ronaldo | Portugal ⬛ | Manchester United
2009	Lionel Messi | Argentina ⤨ | FC Barcelona
2010	Lionel Messi | Argentina ⤨ | FC Barcelona
2011	**Lionel Messi | Argentina ⤨ | FC Barcelona**
2012	Lionel Messi | Argentina ⤨ | FC Barcelona
2013	Cristiano Ronaldo | Portugal ⬛ | Real Madrid
2014	Cristiano Ronaldo | Portugal ⬛ | Real Madrid
2015	Lionel Messi | Argentina ⤨ | FC Barcelona
2016	Cristiano Ronaldo | Portugal ⬛ | Real Madrid
2017	Cristiano Ronaldo | Portugal ⬛ | Real Madrid
2018	Luka Modrić | Croatia | Real Madrid
2019	Lionel Messi | Argentina ⤨ | FC Barcelona
2020	Not Awarded (COVID-19)
Tally of Awards	Messi ⤨ = 6 | Ronaldo ⬛ = 5

FUN FACT From 2008 to 2017, Messi and Ronaldo shared the Ballon d'Or spotlight equally — five wins each. A full decade of back-and-forth brilliance!

Even when cameras caught them chatting and laughing together before big matches, you could see the respect in their eyes. They knew they were witnessing something historic every time they faced each other. Their competition didn't just make them both legends, it gave the world some of the most incredible soccer moments ever played.

You don't need a huge stadium to feel that spark. Maybe you and a team-mate both want to be the top scorer this season, or you and your best friend love testing each other's skills during drills. That little push helps you stay motivated and helps them too. *Healthy rivalries aren't about bringing someone down, they're about pushing each other to rise.*

This kind of friendly challenge appears outside soccer, too. Racing to see who can finish homework first, competing for the highest quiz score, or challenging each other to learn new skills faster. These mini competitions help you focus, work harder, and celebrate each other's progress.

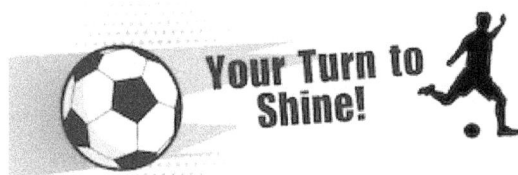

Reflection: My Friendly Rival

Think about a friendly competitor in your life, someone who pushes you to be better:

1. **Who is your friendly rival** — teammate, sibling, classmate?

2. **What do you compete about** — skills, grades, games?

3. **How do they make you better?** Write one specific way they've helped you improve.

How can you encourage them this week? Plan one way to lift them up while still competing.

Remember: ***Real rivals lift each other up***. That's the kind of teammate and friend you want to be.

Beyond the Field

Soccer teaches lessons that stick with you long after the game ends, *resilience* to get back up, *confidence* to try again, *discipline* to keep practicing, *sportsmanship* to show *kindness,* and *friendship* that makes every match sweeter. These lessons come with you into class, into your hobbies, and into every part of your day.

Next, we'll explore how soccer brings people together from every corner of the world. Different countries, different chants, but the same love for the game. Get ready for stories that show how soccer speaks *every language.*

CHAPTER 7: ONE GAME, MANY CULTURES

"Soccer is the only sport that actually stops wars."

— Didier Drogba, Ivorian football legend

S occer isn't just a game. It's a language spoken in every corner of the globe. It brings people together, sparks national pride, and reflects the spirit of entire cultures. In this chapter, we'll take you on a journey across continents to see how the beautiful game looks, feels, and sounds in different parts of the world.

You'll discover why soccer in **Africa** is more than just competition. It's a celebration bursting with music, dance, and community spirit. Then we'll fly to **South America,** where creativity and flair turn every match into a festival of passion and bold moves. Across **Europe,** you'll see how strategy and deep-rooted traditions have shaped the modern game, producing rivalries and legends that fans never forget. In **Asia**, we'll explore how emerging stars and growing leagues are lighting up the fields and inspiring millions of new fans.

Soccer shows us that what unites us can be stronger than what divides us. The way people play might look different from country to country, but the joy, teamwork, and passion are the same. So open your mind, stay curious, and get ready to explore how the world plays, celebrates, and connects through the beautiful game.

7.1 Soccer Around the World

Kick a ball almost anywhere on Earth, and chances are someone will join in. Soccer speaks a language everyone understands, even if they don't share a single word. From busy city streets to quiet village fields, this game brings people together in ways few things can.

FIFA, the organization that oversees global soccer, helps maintain fairness across countries. Every four years, it hosts the FIFA World Cup, a tournament so big that millions of fans cheer from all corners of the globe. For many countries, just qualifying is a dream come true. Winning it? That's pure magic.

What makes the game even more exciting is how each country plays with its own unique style:

- **Brazil** brings rhythm and creativity. Players move with flair, dribbling as if the ball is dancing with them. During big games, fans celebrate with samba music, turning stadiums into full-blown parties.

- **Italy** is known for defence-first strategies. Their classic style, known as *Catenaccio* (meaning "*door-bolt*" in Italian), is all about locking down the field so that no one can score easily.

- **Germany** thrives on precision and discipline. Their teams pass with purpose, always one step ahead. It's like watching a masterclass in timing and teamwork.

These differences are what make international matches so fun to watch. It's not just country versus country. It's style versus style.

But soccer is more than how it's played. It's how it brings people together. One powerful example is **South Africa's** story. When **Nelson Mandela** became president after decades of division, he used sports to help heal his country. While he famously turned to rugby, his message rang true for soccer too: *sports can unite.*

Today, soccer teams around the world take that message seriously. They speak up against racism, stand up for equality, and use their platforms to call for change. Whether on the field or in interviews, many players remind us that teamwork matters just as much off the pitch.

As we saw in the last chapter, when Spain's biggest teams**, Real Madrid** and **FC Barcelona**, battle it out in **El Clásico**, it's more than just a soccer match. It's a showdown that makes hearts pound and voices rise. One clever pass or sudden strike can flip the game in seconds. And the excitement doesn't stay in the stadium. It spreads to living rooms, schoolyards, and streets around the world, where fans of all ages feel part of the action.

At the World Cup, that excitement multiplies. Teams don't just compete for a trophy, they carry the hopes of their nations. A single win can lift spirits, spark celebrations, and bring people closer together.

Your Turn to Shine!

Design Your Dream Kit

Soccer teams from different countries have unique uniforms that reflect their culture. Now it's your turn.

1. **Create your own dream jersey.**

2. **What colors would you use?**

3. **Would it have a logo, slogan, or flag?**

4. **What country or region inspires your design?**

Use crayons, markers, or colored pencils and don't forget to give your team a name! Share your design with friends or family and ask them to create their own.

7.2 Africa's Joyful Game

In the heart of busy streets in Lagos, **Nigeria,** and the sunny fields of Johannesburg, **South Africa,** you'll find one thing in common: kids and adults playing soccer wherever there's space. It might be a dusty road, a school yard, or even a beach. Soccer isn't just a game here. It's part of everyday life.

When a match kicks off, the whole neighbourhood comes alive. There's music, laughter, dancing, and cheering that can shake the ground. During the **Africa Cup of Nations**, one of the continent's biggest tournaments, fans paint their faces, wave colorful flags, and sing for their teams. The competition is a full-on celebration of pride and community.

African teams are known for their bold and exciting style. Players combine quick feet, smart moves, and incredible creativity. They dribble with flair, pass with power, and score in ways that leave the crowd roaring. Watching a match is like watching a dance, fast, fun, and full of surprises.

But soccer in Africa is about more than what happens on the field. It's a way to lift communities and create change. Across the continent, local soccer programs are helping kids attend school, learn teamwork, and build confidence. Groups like *Right to Play* utilize soccer to impart important life lessons and inspire young people to dream big. These programs show that the game isn't just about winning. It's about growing, learning, and believing in yourself.

Some African soccer stars have taken that spirit even further. **Didier Drogba**, from **Ivory Coast**, wasn't just a legend on the pitch. He used his fame to help bring peace during a time of civil war. People listened when he spoke, and that made a real difference.

George Weah, another great from **Liberia**, had one of the most amazing journeys of all. He started out as a kid who loved soccer, became one of the best players in the world, and then went on to become the *president of his country*. His story proves that soccer can take you farther than you ever imagined, not just to big stadiums, but into the history books.

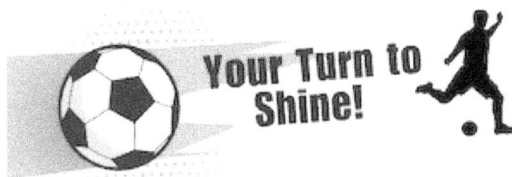
Your Turn to Shine!

Make Your Dream Card

What's a big dream you'd love to reach one day? Maybe it's playing for your country, helping your community, becoming a coach, or starting your own team. Let's turn that dream into something you can see and hold!

Here's how:

1. Grab a blank index card or a small piece of paper (or use the one provided in this book).

2. At the top, write: My dream is...

3. Write or draw your dream provided with this book. Make it as bold, bright, or detailed as you want!

4. On the back, write one thing you can do this week to take a small step toward that dream.

5. Keep your card somewhere special, like in your locker, your journal, or next to your bed, so you can look at it whenever you need a boost.

Your dream matters. Every goal you score, every challenge you face, and every bit of effort you give helps you grow stronger. Just like the soccer heroes who inspired change, you have the power to shape your own future.

MY DREAM CARD

D R E A M   C A R D

Name: _____ Today's date: _____

My dream is: _____

Draw your dream:

I will work towards my dream by:

_____

_____

_____

✂ -

D R E A M   C A R D

Name: _____ Today's date: _____

My dream is: _____

Draw your dream:

I will work towards my goal by:

_____

_____

_____

7.3 Soccer with South American Swagger

In South America, soccer is not just a game. It's a way of life. Imagine waking up in **Buenos Aires** or **Rio de Janeiro** and hearing the sound of a ball being kicked around. Kids play in the streets and on beaches, dreaming of becoming the next big soccer star. Street soccer and *futsal* courts are everywhere, serving as playgrounds where talent is born. The atmosphere is electric, filled with laughter and cheers. Soccer is more than a pastime; it's part of the culture, as essential as breathing or eating.

The soccer matches in **South America** are like no other. Imagine stepping into a stadium where the crowd is buzzing like a beehive. Fans wave flags and sing anthems with all their might. Every goal feels like a carnival, complete with dancing and fireworks. The passion and intensity are unmatched, making every game an unforgettable experience. It's not just about winning; it's about showing love for the team and pride in their country.

South American teams are famous for their skillful and flamboyant style. Brazilian players move with grace, like they're doing the samba on the field. Their samba style is all about flair, making it look like the ball dances with them. In **Argentina**, players use *gambetta* to dazzle opponents, weaving through defenders with tricky dribbles and fancy footwork. The focus is on creativity and attack, keeping fans on the edge of their seats. It's all about expressing individuality and flair on the field.

But soccer in South America isn't just about the pros and the famous. It's also about the *everyday joy* it brings to people's lives. Let me tell you what that looked like during my visits to Bolivia — a country where soccer isn't just a pastime, it's part of the heartbeat of the community.

Real-Life Snapshot: Soccer in Bolivia

While on a work trip to Cochabamba, Bolivia, I was invited to join a friendly match with the women's soccer club at Jalasoft, the tech company I was visiting. It wasn't just a quick kickaround—this was a real match, complete with warm-ups, laughter, and post-game hotdogs. We played on a small field near one of the employees' condos. Even though I was only there for a short time, the game made me feel instantly welcomed. We didn't need to speak the same language—soccer did the talking.

A warm welcome to Bolivia through soccer.

A few years later, I went back to Bolivia for a short mission trip. During a break in our schedule, our group of Canadian missionaries headed to Estadio Félix Capriles to watch a professional match featuring Club Jorge Wilstermann. The crowd was electric—flags waving, confetti flying, and fans of all ages on their feet. Decked out in red-and-blue team colors, we cheered, laughed, and took photos together. It didn't matter where we were from—we were united by the joy of the game.

Cheering with thousands at Estadio Félix Capriles—pure joy!

Soccer in Bolivia doesn't just live on local fields or professional stadiums—it thrives in the hearts of its people. One former colleague, Elmer, proudly shared a photo holding a trophy after his team clinched a tournament victory. He also reminded me that **Bolivia** once reached the world stage: the **1994 FIFA World Cup**. Back then, heroes like Marco Antonio Etcheverry wore the green jersey with pride, and fans packed **Estadio Hernando Siles** in La Paz—one of the world's highest-altitude stadiums at an altitude of 3582m above sea level—to cheer their national team. The energy of that era still echoes in the music, the crowds, and the confetti-filled skies of every match day.

From neighborhood trophies to the 1994 World Cup—soccer is Bolivia's heartbeat. Photos courtesy of Mr. Elmer Alvarado, Cochabamba, Bolivia. Used with permission.

Estadio Hernando Siles in La Paz, sits at a breathtaking 3,582 meters (11,750 feet) above sea level — making it one of the **highest-altitude stadiums** in the world! Visiting teams often find it hard to breathe... but Bolivian players are used to it and play like champs.

Stories like those from Bolivia remind us that soccer's role in South America extends beyond entertainment; it is deeply tied to national identity and pride. The World Cup is a big deal here. When their team plays, the whole country stops to watch together. A win can lift spirits and unite people like nothing else. Historical rivalries, like **Brazil** versus **Argentina**, are intense. These matches go beyond sports; they're about history and pride. They create legendary moments that fans remember forever.

South America has given us some of the greatest soccer players in history. **Pelé**, from **Brazil**, isn't just a legend; he's an ambassador for the sport worldwide. His influence reaches far beyond the field, inspiring millions to pick up a ball and dream big. Then there's **Diego Maradona** from **Argentina.** With quick feet and a fierce spirit, he became a cultural icon. His name is synonymous with passion and skill, leaving a legacy that endures through generations.

These legends have left an indelible mark on soccer's history. **Pelé** made magic happen on the field with his dazzling goals and charisma. **Maradona**'s iconic moments continue to inspire young players everywhere to chase their dreams. Their stories teach us about dedication, talent, and the power of soccer to change lives.

South American soccer is a celebration of life itself. It reflects not just talent but also dreams, pride, and unity among people who share a love for the game. So, whether you're dribbling in your backyard or watching a thrilling match on TV, remember that you're part of something much bigger. This beautiful game connects us all with joy and passion.

Your Turn to Shine!

Create Your Own Flair Move

South American soccer is characterized by its flair, fun, and intricate footwork. Now it's your turn to add some spice to the game, right where you are!

Here's what to do:

1. **Invent a move:** Come up with your own unique soccer trick or footwork move. It could be a spin, a feint, a cool juggling trick, anything that feels fun and flashy. Give it a fun name too!

2. **Practice it:** Grab a ball and practice your move a few times until you've got it down. Show it off to a sibling, friend, or teammate and teach them how to do it too.

3. **Add some music:** South American soccer celebrates rhythm and creativity. Put on a fun song and try your move in time with the beat, like you're dancing with the ball!

4. **Journal prompt (optional):** Write about how it felt to invent your own move. Did it make you feel confident? Did it make soccer more fun? Would you use it in a real game?

Every time you play, you're telling a story, your story. Pelé did it with joy. Maradona did it with fire. Maybe your move is next. So keep creating, keep dreaming, and keep dancing with the ball.

7.4 European Strategy and Tradition

Think of a soccer field like a giant puzzle. Every player is a piece that has to move with purpose, and when those pieces click into place, you get something magical.

In **Germany**, strategy meets precision. Teams focus on *efficiency,* where every pass, move, and shot is carefully planned and executed. It's like watching a well-rehearsed routine where everyone knows their role. German soccer is renowned for its strong teamwork and rapid counterattacks that strike at just the right moment.

Now take a look at **Spain**. Spanish teams are famous for a style called *tiki-taka*, a quick-passing game that keeps the ball constantly moving. It's like watching the ball play keep-away, zipping from one player to another in short, sharp passes. The goal? Wear out the other team and then slip in the perfect shot. It's clever, smooth, and full of rhythm, like dancing with the ball.

And over in the **Netherlands**, there's *total football*. In this strategy, players can switch positions at any moment. Defenders might suddenly attack, and attackers drop back to defend. Everyone's expected to know every role on the field. It's flexible, exciting, and super smart, like a shape-shifting team always one step ahead.

In Europe, the magic isn't only crafted by the players on the pitch. It's carried by the fans who fill the stands with songs, banners, and unstoppable energy. Step into a stadium in England, and you'll hear roaring chants that echo through history. In **Italy,** fans bring drums and banners, transforming games into a living art form. And in **Turkey**, matches light up with fireworks and songs that keep going long after the final whistle. Each crowd adds its own heartbeat, making European soccer feel electric, passionate, and larger than life.

European club competitions are like soccer's biggest stage shows. The **UEFA Champions League** is where top teams compete for glory. It's like the *Oscars of soccer*! Clubs from all over Europe battle it out in thrilling matches that showcase talent and skill. These games set trends and inspire players worldwide. And then there's the **English Premier League**, one of the most-watched leagues globally. It's known for its fast-paced games and diverse talent pool. Players from every corner of the earth dream of playing here.

Many of these tactical styles were shaped by soccer masterminds. **Johan Cruyff** helped revolutionize **Total Football** in the **Netherlands**, and **Franz Beckenbauer** redefined the defender's role in Germany. You'll learn more about both of these legends in Chapter 10.

European soccer is a blend of tactics, talent, and tradition. It's where new ideas bloom and old ones find new life. Every game is an adventure filled with excitement and skill. Whether it's an Italian team building an impenetrable defence or a Spanish side weaving intricate patterns with their passes, European soccer offers something special for every fan to enjoy.

Your Turn to Shine!

Build Your Dream Team Strategy!

You're the coach now! Europe is full of creative styles and clever strategies, so let's mix things up and build your own custom game plan.

1. Choose your style
Pick one of these soccer styles for your team:

- Tiki-taka (Spain): short, quick passes to keep the ball moving

- Total Football (Netherlands): players can switch positions anytime

- Counterattack Power (Germany): solid teamwork with surprise strikes

2. Draw your formation.
Grab a blank piece of paper and sketch a simple soccer field. Place your players where you think they should start. Do you want more defenders? Extra attackers? You decide!

3. Create a signature move.
Invent one cool "team move" your squad will use. Maybe it's a sneaky back-pass, a tricky fake-out, or a powerful long shot. Give it a fun name!

4. Share and compare.
Show your strategy to a friend or sibling and ask about theirs. Would your styles work well together, or would it be an epic face-off?

Soccer isn't just about playing. It's about thinking, planning, and creating magic on the field. With your own strategy in place, you're already thinking like a soccer legend!

7.5 Rising Stars in Asian Soccer

Across Asia, soccer is taking center stage. Countries like **Japan** and **South Korea** are showing the world they mean business in soccer. Japan has won hearts with their impressive performance in the **AFC Asian Cup**. They've shown everyone that they're a force to be reckoned with. South Korea, on the other hand, has made waves in the **FIFA World Cup**. They surprised everyone by reaching the semifinals in 2002. This made them one of the first Asian countries to achieve such success. Both countries continue to build strong teams and nurture young talent. It's exciting to see how they're shaping the world of soccer.

But it's not just about playing the game. Across Asia, there's a big push to improve soccer infrastructure. Governments and private companies are investing time and money into building better facilities. Soccer academies are popping up everywhere. These academies are like superhero training camps for young players. They focus on developing skills and teaching kids how to play like pros. With shiny new training centers and considerable effort, Asia is cultivating a new generation of talented players poised to take on the world.

Soccer is also becoming a significant part of Asian culture. Local leagues, such as the **J League** in Japan and the **K League** in South Korea, are receiving considerable attention. Matches are no longer just games; they're events that bring communities together. Fans fill stadiums to cheer for their favorite teams and enjoy the electric atmosphere.

Asian players are also making their mark on the international stage. **Park Ji-sung** is one example of a true trailblazer. He was one of the first Asian players to succeed in European soccer, playing for **Manchester United.** His dedication and hard work opened doors for other Asian players to follow their dreams. Then there's **Sunil Chhetri** from **India**, who has become an icon in his country's soccer scene. His leadership and skill have inspired many young players to pick up a ball and start playing.

As we examine the progress of Asian soccer, it's clear that they're not only playing but competing. The investment in infrastructure, focus on developing talent, and cultural embrace of soccer have all contributed to this growth. Asia is stepping onto the global soccer stage with confidence and enthusiasm, ready to showcase its capabilities.

Your Turn to Shine!

Design an Asian Soccer Super Academy!

Soccer in Asia is growing fast, with new academies, cool stadiums, and rising stars. Now it's your turn to help shape the future!

1. Build your soccer academy.
Grab a sheet of paper and sketch your very own *Soccer Super Academy*. What does it look like? Add: a) The name for your academy, b)Training fields (how many?), c) A locker room or clubhouse, d) A fan zone for cheering families e) A cool logo or team mascot

2. Pick your star coaches.
Choose 2–3 soccer players from Asia you'd want as coaches. Maybe Park Ji-sung for speed and teamwork, or Sunil Chhetri for leadership. What would they teach young players?

3. Create a training plan.
List 3 fun drills or lessons you'd include in your academy: a)A passing challenge?, b) A penalty kick showdown? c) A teamwork obstacle course?

4. Invite your friends. Who would you invite to join? Write down names of friends or classmates you'd train with. What would your team be called?

Asia's soccer scene is on fire, and now you're part of it! With your own academy, you're helping shape the next generation of players, just like a real soccer legend!

As we come to the end of this chapter, think about what soccer looks like around the world. In every country, it takes on a different rhythm and meaning. Some play with flair, others with strategy. But no matter where you go, the game has unifying power. From Africa's joyful dances to Asia's rising stars, soccer reflects the heart of the people who play it. That's what makes it unforgettable.

In the next chapter, we'll relive some of the most unforgettable moments in soccer history and reflect on what they teach us about *courage, unity,* and *perseverance*. Get ready for the stories, celebrations, and lessons that make the beautiful game truly legendary.

Chapter 8: Goals, Glory, and Grit

I've never scored a goal in my life without getting a pass from someone else.

—Abby Wambach

S ome soccer moments are so powerful they become part of history, not just for the goals scored but for the emotions, surprises, and lessons they bring. In this final chapter, we'll relive some of the game's most unforgettable highs, heart-stopping comebacks, and inspiring victories that taught the world what's possible when you believe.

You'll journey to **Brazil in 1970**, where a team turned soccer into poetry. We'll witness **Denmark**'s impossible fairy tale in **1992**, celebrate **Aguero**'s last-second magic in **2012**, and marvel at **Leicester City's** dream that defied all odds. These aren't just famous plays and wins, they're stories about **courage, teamwork, resilience**, and the **power of never giving up**.

Because sometimes, the moments that stay with us the longest aren't just about soccer. They're about life, hope, and daring to believe in the impossible.

8.1 Brazil 1970: When Soccer Became Poetry

Mexico, 1970. The World Cup is being broadcast in color for the first time, and the world is about to witness something magical. Brazil's team didn't just play soccer but also painted masterpieces on the pitch. With **Pelé** leading the way, alongside **Carlos Alberto**, **Jairzinho**, and **Tostão**, they moved like dancers and struck like lightning.

But here's what made them special: they played with *pure joy*. While other teams focused on not losing, Brazil focused on creating beauty. They passed the ball like it was a conversation between best friends. They celebrated each other's skills as much as their own goals. When Carlos Alberto scored the final goal in the World Cup final, a flowing move that involved nearly the entire team, it was art in its finest!

The Brazilian players came from different backgrounds across their vast country. Some grew up poor, others middle-class, but on the field, they moved as one. They proved that when you combine individual brilliance with selfless teamwork, magic happens. Their 4–1 victory over Italy in the World Cup Final showed the world how joyful, creative, and powerful soccer can be when a team plays with heart.

What shocked the world wasn't just their skill, but their *attitude*. After scoring spectacular goals, they'd immediately look for a teammate to hug. They played like they were having the time of their lives, and that joy was contagious. Fans who had never cared about soccer suddenly understood why it was called "*the beautiful game*."

Brazil in 1970 didn't just win a World Cup. They changed how the world saw the game. Their joy was genuine, their teamwork effortless, and their style unforgettable. They reminded everyone that excellence can be playful, and that greatness doesn't always wear a serious face. When players lift each other up and play together with heart, the game is simply beautiful.

Your Turn to Shine!

Your Beautiful Game Challenge

Brazil 1970 showed that the most powerful moments come from combining individual talent with team joy. Time to create your own beautiful moment!

Step 1: Design Your Dream Play
- Draw or write about an amazing team play (in soccer, at school, or anywhere)

- Show how each person's unique skill contributes to something bigger

- Include the celebration, how does your team show joy together?

Step 2: The Joy Factor
- List 3 things that make playing/working with others fun for you

- Write one way you can bring more joy to your next team activity

- Design a "Beautiful Game Badge" that represents playing with both skill and happiness

Step 3: Share the Magic
- Teach someone a skill you're good at, just like Brazil players shared their talents

- Plan a group activity where everyone gets to shine

Remember: The most beautiful victories happen when everyone's individual magic combines into something even more amazing!

8.2 Denmark 1992: The Ultimate Last-Minute Heroes

Sometimes the most incredible stories begin with the words "*You weren't even supposed to be here*." That's exactly what happened to **Denmark in 1992**. They weren't originally invited to the **European Championship**, **Yugoslavia** was supposed to play, but due to political conflict, they were banned just 10 days before the tournament started.

Denmark's players were literally on vacation. Some were painting their houses, others were relaxing on beaches. Then came the phone call: "*Pack your boots. You're going to Sweden.*" Most people thought Denmark would be knocked out quickly. After all, they'd had almost no time to prepare, no training camp, and low expectations.

But sometimes, magic happens when the pressure is off.

Denmark didn't have the most famous players or the fanciest tactics. What they had was something more powerful: *nothing to lose and everything to prove*. They played with freedom, taking risks and supporting each other through every challenge. When they reached the final against heavily favored Germany, the fairy tale seemed complete, except they still had to win.

In a tense final, Denmark's goalkeeper made incredible saves, their defense stood firm, and their attackers found moments of brilliance. The final score: Denmark 2, Germany 0. The players who had been painting houses two weeks earlier were now European champions, dancing on the field in disbelief.

The Danish players later said the secret was simple: *they played for each other, not for glory*. When opportunity knocked at the last minute, they were ready. They proved that sometimes the best preparation for success is simply being willing to say "*yes*" when the chance comes.

Denmark 1992 reminds us that extraordinary opportunities can appear when we least expect them and the key is being ready to seize them with both hands.

Your Turn to Shine!

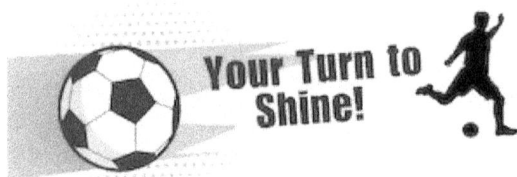

Your Last-Minute Opportunity Challenge

Denmark taught us that amazing chances can come out of nowhere and the secret is being ready to grab them!

Step 1: Opportunity Radar

- Think of a time when an unexpected chance came your way (getting picked for something, a friend asking for help, a surprise invitation)

- How did you react? What happened?

- Write about a current opportunity you might be overlooking

Step 2: Ready Player One

- List 3 skills or qualities you have that prepare you for surprise opportunities

- Design an "Always Ready" kit, what would you need to be prepared for unexpected awesome moments?

- Practice saying "*Yes, I can try that!*" out loud (seriously, practice it!)

Step 3: Create Your Opportunity

- Look around: is there a friend, classmate, or family member who could use some help or support?

- Be someone else's "unexpected opportunity" this week

- Plan one small thing you can do to create a surprise positive moment for others

Bonus Challenge: Make an "*Opportunity Alert*" poster with the message: "*When chance knocks, I'm ready!*" Hang it where you'll see it daily. Remember: Like Denmark's players, **you never know when your moment will come, but when it does, you'll be ready!**

8.3 Aguero 2012: The Goal That Stopped Time

May 13, 2012. **Manchester City vs. Queens Park Rangers.** The **Premier League** title was on the line, and Manchester City needed to win. But with just minutes left, they were losing 2-1. Their fans were devastated. Some had even started leaving the stadium, thinking their dream season was over.

Then, something extraordinary happened.

In the 92nd minute, deep into stoppage time, **Edin Dzeko** scored to tie the game 2-2. The stadium erupted, but it wasn't enough. Manchester City still needed another goal to win the title. The clock was ticking. Seconds felt like hours.

93rd minute, 20 seconds. The ball came to **Sergio Aguero** inside the penalty box. Defenders rushed toward him. The weight of an entire season, an entire city's hopes, rested on his shoulders. Time seemed to freeze.

Aguero took one touch, then another. He shifted the ball to his left foot and unleashed a shot into the bottom corner of the net. GOAL! The stadium exploded. Fans hugged strangers. Players collapsed in joy. At that moment, Aguero had delivered **Manchester City** their *first league title in 44 years*.

But here's what made it truly special: Aguero later revealed he almost gave up in that final moment. His legs were tired, his mind was screaming "*It's over*," but something inside him said "*Try one more time*." That "one more time" changed *everything*.

The announcer's famous words captured the magic: "*Aguero! I swear you'll never see anything like this ever again!*" And maybe we won't. But Aguero's goal teaches us something powerful: the biggest breakthroughs often come when we think we have nothing left to give.

That goal wasn't just about skill. It was about heart, grit, and pushing forward when everything seemed lost. The biggest victories often come in those final seconds, when you choose to keep going. So the next time you feel like giving up, remember this moment. One extra effort might be the one that changes everything.

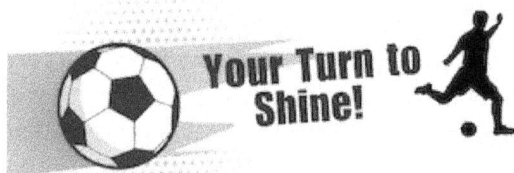

Your Turn to Shine!

Your Final-Second Victory Challenge

Aguero showed us that magic happens when we keep trying even when everything seems lost. Time to discover your own "*never give up*" power!

Step 1: Your Aguero Moment
- Think of a time when you almost gave up but decided to try "one more time"

- What happened? How did it feel to push through?

- Draw or write about that moment when you found strength you didn't know you had

Step 2: Build Your Mental Toughness Toolkit
- Create 3 "power phrases" you can tell yourself when things get tough (like "*One more try*" or "*I'm stronger than I think*")

- Design a "*Never Quit*" symbol you can draw on your hand before challenges

- Practice your "final push" celebration, how will you celebrate when you don't give up?

Step 3: The 93rd Minute Challenge

- This week, when you feel like quitting something (home-work, practice, a difficult conversation), give it "one more try"

- Help someone else find their "final push" when they want to give up

- Keep track of your "Aguero moments", times when you kept going when it was hard

Bonus Power Move: Set a timer for 93 seconds and practice doing something challenging (like juggling a ball, solving a puzzle, or writing) right up until the final second. Feel that "final push" energy!

Remember: ***Your biggest victories might be waiting just one more try away!***

8.4 Leicester City 2015-16: When Dreams Defied Reality

The odds were 5,000 to 1. That means you were more likely to spot Elvis working at your local grocery store than to see **Leicester City** win the **Premier League**. But sometimes, the most impossible dreams are just waiting for the right team to believe in them.

Leicester City wasn't supposed to be champions. They'd almost been relegated (kicked out of the Premier League) the season before. Their players weren't superstars and most other teams don't even want them. **Jamie Vardy** had been playing in lower leagues just a few years earlier. **N'Golo Kanté** was relatively unknown. **Riyad Mahrez** was considered too small for the Premier League.

But Leicester had something more valuable than famous names: *they had each other.*

Manager **Claudio Ranieri** created a family atmosphere where every player felt valued. When Vardy went on an incredible scoring streak, the whole team celebrated like they'd all scored. When Kanté made his tireless runs up and down the field, covering more ground than anyone thought possible, his teammates fed off his energy. When Mahrez dazzled opponents with his skills, the others created space for his magic.

The team was beautifully *diverse* with players from **England, France, Algeria, Japan**, and many other countries, all united by one crazy dream. They proved that you don't need the most expensive players; you need players who *believe* in each other completely.

As the season progressed, other teams started panicking when they played Leicester, because they realized these "*underdogs*" genuinely believed they could win. That belief became contagious. The fans believed. The city believed. Soon, the whole world was cheering for them.

When Leicester clinched the title, players cried tears of joy. Families in Leicester threw street parties. People who'd never watched soccer before were suddenly fans. Leicester City had proved that with enough *heart, teamwork,* and *unwavering belief*, even the most impossible dreams can come true.

Leicester's story wasn't just a sports surprise. It was a reminder that belief can be stronger than odds, and teamwork louder than doubt. When a group of players trust each other and play with heart, they can turn a long shot into a legend.

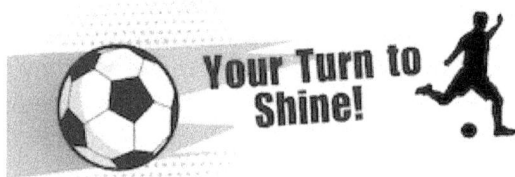

Your Impossible Dream Challenge

Leicester City proved that no dream is too big when you have the right team and unshakeable belief. Time to unlock your own impossible!

Step 1: Dream Without Limits

- Write down one dream that feels "impossible" to you right now

- Break it into smaller pieces, what would the first step look like?

- Design your "5000-to-1" victory celebration, how would you celebrate making the impossible happen?

Step 2: Build Your Leicester City Team
- List the people who believe in your dreams (family, friends, coaches, teachers)

- Identify one person whose dream you can support this week

- Create a "Dream Team" plan, how can you and your supporters help each other achieve impossible things?

Step 3: The Belief Training
- Every morning for one week, look in the mirror and say: "Impossible is just a word"

- When someone says "that's too hard" or "you can't do that," smile and think of Leicester City

- Start a "Small Victories" journal, track daily wins that prove you're capable of more than you think

Step 4: Your Leicester Moment
- Choose one "impossible" thing to attempt this month (learning a new skill, making a new friend, improving at something you struggle with)

- Document your journey, the setbacks, the breakthroughs, the moments of doubt, and the celebrations

- Share your story with someone else who has a big dream

The Leicester City Reminder Card: Create a small card that says "5000-to-1 odds didn't stop them" and keep it with you. When things feel impossible, remember the team that proved impossible is just the starting point for something magical.

Remember: *Every impossible dream is just waiting for someone brave enough to believe it's possible!*

8.5 Making Your Own Iconic Moment

You've journeyed through Brazil's joyful artistry, Denmark's last-minute miracle, Aguero's never-give-up spirit, and Leicester's impossible dream. These weren't just soccer moments, they were lessons about what humans can achieve when we play with joy, seize opportunities, refuse to quit, and dare to dream big.

But here's the most important part: *your own iconic moment is waiting to be written.*

It might not happen in a stadium filled with thousands of fans. It could happen in your backyard, at school, or anywhere you choose to show **courage, kindness,** or **determination**. The magic isn't in the size of the stage. It's in the size of your heart and the strength of your spirit.

Brazil 1970 reminds us to find joy in working together. **Denmark 1992** teaches us to be ready when opportunity knocks. **Aguero 2012** shows us the power of one more try. **Leicester 2015-16** proves that no dream is too impossible.

These moments became legendary because they revealed something beautiful about the human spirit. They showed us that ordinary people can do extraordinary things when they believe in themselves and support each other.

Your iconic moment might be the day you help a teammate who's struggling, the time you score your first goal, the moment you stand up for someone being treated unfairly, or the day you achieve something everyone said was impossible for you.

The world is waiting for your story. What will it be?

This concludes our journey through soccer's most iconic moments and the life lessons they teach. We've seen how the beautiful game can inspire us to play with joy, seize unexpected opportunities, never give up in crucial moments, and believe in dreams that seem impossible.

These stories remind us that greatness isn't reserved for professional athletes in famous stadiums. It lives inside every person who chooses courage over comfort, teamwork over individual glory, and hope over doubt.

Next, we'll shift gears completely and dive into the lighter side of soccer. Get ready for laughs, surprises, and the wonderfully weird moments that remind us why we fell in love with this beautiful, unpredictable game in the first place!

Chapter 9: Funny Moments on the Field

"We lost because we didn't win."

— *Ronaldo Nazário, legendary Brazilian striker*

Soccer is full of passion, discipline, and unforgettable victories, but it's also packed with laughter, playful moments, and silly surprises that remind us why we love the game in the first place. In this chapter, we'll explore the funny, unexpected, and joyful side of soccer that even the most prominent stars can't resist.

You'll giggle at famous bloopers where pros trip, slip, or miss in ways that prove everyone makes mistakes, and that it's okay to laugh and keep going. We'll peek inside locker rooms where pranks and playful tricks bring teams closer together. You'll see why scoring a goal often leads to wild dances, silly moves, and celebrations that become as legendary as the goals themselves. And through it all, we'll remember that while winning feels great, having fun and loving what you do are what really keep players coming back to the pitch.

Soccer teaches us to try hard, work together, and aim high, but it also reminds us to smile, laugh at our stumbles, and celebrate every moment. Because sometimes, the best memories aren't the perfect passes. They're the moments when we're just being ourselves, sharing joy with teammates and fans alike!

9.1 Famous Bloopers: When Soccer Gets Silly

Even the world's greatest soccer players have moments that make everyone burst out laughing. These funny fails remind us that mistakes happen to everyone and that's perfectly okay!

When the Ball Has a Mind of Its Own

Liverpool's **Steven Gerrard**, one of England's most respected captains, slipping at the worst possible moment during a crucial match against Chelsea. It was 2014, and Liverpool was so close to winning their first Premier League title in 24 years. But sometimes, even heroes slip on the grass! Gerrard lost his footing, Chelsea scored, and Liverpool's title dreams slipped away. But you know what? Gerrard laughed about it later and kept being an amazing player and leader.

Or how about when Germany's goalkeeper **Oliver Kahn**, known as one of the fiercest, most serious keepers ever, accidentally threw the ball directly to Brazil's Ronaldo during the 2002 World Cup final? Kahn's face when he realized what happened was priceless! Even he had to chuckle about it afterward.

David Beckham's Penalty Oops

Think of **David Beckham**, one of the coolest soccer legends ever. In a 2004 European Championship match against France, he stepped up to take a penalty kick that could help England advance. Everyone was holding their breath. But instead of finding the net, Beckham's shot sailed way over the crossbar and into the stands! The cameras caught his surprised expression, and even Beckham had to smile and shrug. That's what makes him a true champion. He could laugh at himself and keep playing with confidence.

Carli Lloyd's Wild Shot

Even World Cup champions have funny moments! **Carli Lloyd** from the US women's team once attempted a powerful shot during a friendly match, but instead of flying toward the goal, the ball went completely sideways and nearly bonked a photographer on the sidelines! Lloyd grinned, gave a little wave to the photographer, and kept playing. Her teammates were cracking up, and it became one of their favorite stories to tell.

The Case of the Runaway Cleat

During a Premier League match, **Chelsea's Willian** was sprinting down the wing when his shoe suddenly flew off his foot and sailed through the air like a missile! He had to keep running in his sock while his teammates pointed and laughed. The best part? He still managed to make a great pass before hopping over to retrieve his rogue cleat. Talk about playing through adversity!

What We Learn: These hilarious moments teach us that even the most skilled players in the world make mistakes, and that's totally normal! The real champions are the ones who can laugh at themselves, learn from their oops moments, and keep playing with joy. When you mess up during your next game, remember these stories and don't forget to smile!

Your Turn to Shine!

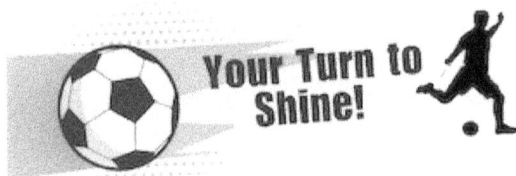

Blooper Challenge!

With your teammates, create your own "*Blooper Hall of Fame*"! Take turns safely acting out funny soccer mistakes (no real falling!):

- The "**invisible banana peel**" slip while dribbling

- The "**super serious**" celebration for scoring in your own goal

- The "**where did the ball go?**" confused look after whiffing a shot

- The "**victory dance**" before realizing you missed the net entirely

Remember: The goal is to laugh together and remember that **mistakes are just part of the game!**

9.2 Pranks and Fun: Locker Room Legends

Step into a professional soccer locker room, and you'll discover that the world's biggest stars are just big kids at heart! The pranks and silly moments that happen behind the scenes help teammates become true friends.

World-Class Pranksters

Wayne Rooney's Jelly Surprise: At Manchester United, **Wayne Rooney** was famous for his cheeky pranks. His favorite target? **Rio Ferdinand**. One morning before training, Rooney filled Rio's expensive boots with strawberry jelly. When Rio slipped his feet in... SQUISH! The whole team erupted in laughter, and even Rio couldn't stay mad, especially when Rooney offered to buy him new boots!

Cristiano Ronaldo's Hide-and-Seek: You might think **Cristiano Ronaldo** is all business, but his Real Madrid teammates knew better. He once hid **Pepe**'s shoes so well that Pepe had to borrow cleats from the equipment manager for warm-ups. When Pepe finally found his shoes hanging from the locker room ceiling, Ronaldo was already giggling like a schoolboy.

Neymar's Sticky Situation: Brazilian star **Neymar** loved a good prank. He once super-glued his Barcelona teammate **Dani Alves's** sandals to the locker room floor. When Alves tried to slip them on and walk away, he nearly face-planted! Both players ended up laughing so hard they had tears streaming down their faces.

Marcelo's Ice Water Ambush: Real Madrid's **Marcelo** was the master of surprise ice water attacks. He'd sneak up on teammates after practice and dump cups of freezing water over their heads. Even serious players like **Sergio Ramos** would jump and yelp like little kids!

What We Learn: These playful moments show us that laughter is like a secret ingredient that makes teams stronger. When players can joke around together, they trust each other more on the field. The teams that laugh together really do stick together!

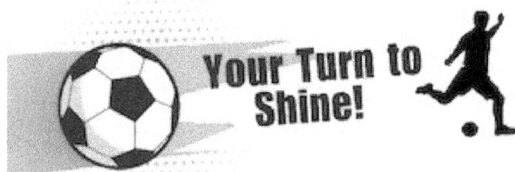

Prank Planning Session!

Ready to spread some giggles with your soccer friends? Here are some harmless ideas:

The Silly Sock Challenge: Everyone wears their socks on their hands during warm-ups and acts completely serious about it.
Googly Eye Invasion: Stick googly eyes on water bottles, cones, or anything that doesn't move. Watch your teammates try not to laugh when everything seems to be watching them!
The Mystery Photo: Print a huge picture of your coach's favorite player and tape it inside someone's locker. Bonus points if it's a funny action shot!
The Backwards Day: Convince your whole team to wear their jerseys backward for warm-ups and see how long it takes the coach to notice.
Remember: The best pranks leave everyone smiling and wanting to be part of the team!

9.3 Goal Celebrations: Dancing Into Soccer History

Scoring a goal feels amazing, but what happens next might be even more fun to watch! Goal celebrations have become as famous as the goals themselves, and they show us that soccer is about expressing joy and personality.

Legendary Celebration Moves

Peter Crouch's Robot Revolution: When England's Peter Crouch scored, he didn't just celebrate, he entertained! This super-tall, serious-looking striker would suddenly break into the most hilarious robot dance you've ever seen! All stiff arms, jerky movements, and mechanical turns. Fans went absolutely crazy for it, and soon kids everywhere were doing the "*Crouch Robot*" in their backyards.

Cristiano Ronaldo's "SIIIIU": Ronaldo's celebration is like a victory cry that the whole stadium joins. He runs to the corner, leaps into the air, spins around, and shouts "SIIIIU!" The crowd roars it back at him. It's become so famous that fans chant it even when he's not playing!

The Icelandic Viking Ship: During the 2016 European Championship, Iceland's players created one of the coolest team celebrations ever. After scoring, they'd line up and pretend to row a Viking longboat, complete with rowing motions and battle chants. It perfectly captured their warrior spirit and national pride.

Megan Rapinoe's Victory Pose: After scoring crucial goals for the US women's team, Megan Rapinoe would stretch her arms wide like she was embracing the entire stadium. Her confident, joyful celebrations showed young girls everywhere that it's awesome to be proud of your achievements.

Celebrations with Heart

Some of the most touching celebrations happen when players dedicate their goals to people they love:

- **Son Heung-min** forms a camera with his hands, pretending to take a photo to capture the moment forever—he says it's for the fans, so they remember the joy.

- **Marcus Rashford** makes a heart with his hands for his mom, who worked multiple jobs to support his soccer dreams.

- **Alex Morgan** pretends to sip tea, a cheeky response to critics who doubted the US women's team.

Son Heung-min, one of the world's top scorers, left home at age 16 to pursue soccer in Germany—even though he didn't speak the language! Today, he played for **Tottenham Hotspurs** in the **Premier League** and in 2025, he brought his talent to the U.S., joining **Los Angeles FC (LAFC)**! Son is also a national hero in South Korea.

In 2018, he helped South Korea win the Asian Games and earned exemption from military service. But get this—he still completed basic training during the pandemic and ranked in the top 5 of his class!

Fans call him "**The Smiling Assassin**" because of his kind heart off the field and sharp skills on it.

When Celebrations Go Viral

Goal celebrations don't stay in the stadium, they explode across the internet! Kids copy them at school, fans turn them into TikTok dances, and suddenly a silly celebration becomes a worldwide phenomenon. Some celebrations become so popular that they're more famous than the goals themselves!

What We Learn: Celebrations teach us that it's important to express joy and be proud of our accomplishments. They also show us that soccer is about more than just scoring. It's about sharing happiness with others and being true to yourself.

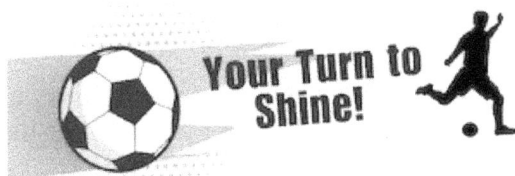

Your Turn to Shine!

Create Your Victory Dance!

Time to invent your own signature celebration! Gather your soccer buddies and try these ideas:

Animal Kingdom:
- The Soaring Eagle (spread your arms and glide)

- The Charging Rhino (put your head down and charge in a circle)

- The Leaping Kangaroo (hop around with joy)

Superhero Squad:
- The Flying Superman (arms stretched forward)

- The Incredible Hulk (flex and roar)

- The Wonder Woman Spin (spin with arms crossed)

Team Celebrations:
- The Human Train (line up and chug around the field)

- The Victory Wave (create a wave motion down the line)

- The Group Hug Explosion (pile on the goal scorer safely!)

The Celebration Championship:
- Take turns showing off your signature moves

- Vote for the funniest, most creative, and most team-spirited celebrations

- Practice them so you're ready for your next goal!

Remember: The best celebrations come from the heart and bring smiles to everyone watching! You've celebrated goals, slipped on grass, and laughed till your belly hurt. But none of those moments would be possible without the people behind the scenes.

Up next, get ready to meet the coaches, mentors, and guiding stars who help shape every soccer story both on and off the field.

Chapter 10: Behind Every Great Player

"The greatest gift I gave my players was to help them see how great they could be."

—Jill Ellis

E ven the greatest soccer stars didn't get there alone. Behind every powerful kick, clever pass, and brave comeback, there's often someone cheering, teaching, and guiding from the sidelines. In this chapter, we'll shine a spotlight on the people who help transform raw talent into true greatness, showing that support, trust, and kindness can make all the difference.

You'll discover the vital role of coaches, not just as teachers of skills and strategies but as leaders who share wisdom, build confidence, and bring out the best in every player. We'll explore how mentors, whether famous athletes or older teammates, can inspire us to keep going and push beyond our limits. And we'll celebrate the special bond between parents and players, where encouragement, patience, and shared excitement help kids grow both on and off the field.

Finally, we'll ask an important question: *Who inspires you*? Because everyone, whether on a big stadium stage or in a local park, can learn from those who've walked the path before, and one day, you might become someone else's guide, too.

10.1 Legendary Coaches: The Game Changers

Great coaches don't just teach you how to kick a ball. They help you *believe* in yourself when you don't think you can do it. Let's meet some of the most amazing coaches who turned ordinary players into superstars.

SIR ALEX
FERGUSON

JILL
ELLIS

PEP
GUARDIOLA

Sir Alex Ferguson: The Master Builder

Imagine walking into **Manchester United**'s training ground as a nervous teenager and meeting **Sir Alex Ferguson**. This Scottish coach had a special power: he could see greatness in players before they even knew it was there.

When **Cristiano Ronaldo** arrived at Manchester United at just 18 years old, he was incredibly talented but also young and sometimes cocky. Ferguson didn't just teach him soccer skills, he taught him how to be a leader. Ferguson would pull Ronaldo aside and say, "*You have a choice: you can be good, or you can be the best player in the world. But that means working harder than everyone else.*"

Ferguson's tough love worked. He helped Ronaldo become more disciplined, more focused, and more determined. Years later, Ronaldo said Ferguson was like a father to him, someone who believed in him even when he made mistakes.

Ferguson won 38 trophies in 26 years at Manchester United, but his real success was in the players he helped grow up. He knew exactly what each player needed. Some needed encouragement, others needed a gentle push, and some needed to be challenged.

Jill Ellis: The Quiet Revolutionary

Jill Ellis might not have been the loudest coach on the sidelines, but her players trusted her completely. When she took over the **US Women's National Team**, she had a big challenge: help them win their first World Cup in 16 years.

Ellis had a special way of making each player feel important. She didn't just focus on the superstars. She made sure every player on the team knew their role and felt valued. During the **2015 World Cup**, when some people criticized her decisions, she stayed calm and confident.

Her player, **Carli Lloyd,** said Ellis had a gift for knowing exactly what to say at the right moment. Before the 2015 World Cup final, Ellis told her team:

"You've worked your whole lives for this moment. Now go out there and show the world who you are."

The team won that World Cup, and then another one in 2019. Ellis proved that great coaching isn't about yelling or being dramatic. Sometimes, it's about *quiet confidence* and making your players *believe* they can conquer the world.

Pep Guardiola: The Perfectionist Artist

Pep Guardiola sees soccer like an artist sees a blank canvas. When he was coaching Barcelona, he took a young **Lionel Messi** and helped turn him into the greatest player many people have ever seen.

Guardiola's secret? He paid attention to tiny details that other coaches missed. He would spend hours showing players exactly where to stand, how to pass, and when to move. During training sessions, he'd stop play to move a player just two steps to the left, explaining how that small change would create a better passing angle. He'd demonstrate how a midfielder could use the inside of their foot instead of the outside to make a pass arrive one second faster, and that one second could be the difference between scoring and losing the ball.

It might sound boring, but his players loved it because they could see how much he cared. During one famous match, **in 2012-2013 UEFA Champions League**, in the first game, Barcelona lost 2–0 to AC Milan. That meant they had to make a huge comeback in the second game to stay in the tournament. Most teams would panic—but not Pep. At halftime, with the score still tied, he calmly told his players,"We're playing perfectly. Keep doing exactly what you're doing."In the second half of that second game, Barcelona scored four amazing goals and won 4–0! Their comeback was so strong that they moved on to the next round. It became one of the most unforgettable moments in Champions League history.

Messi once said:

"Pep taught me to see the game differently. It wasn't just about scoring, it was about creating."

Messi's reflected that Guardiola helped him see soccer not just as a game of goals, but as a way to create something beautiful with others.

What Makes These Coaches Special:

- They see potential in players before the players see it in themselves

- They know how to talk to each player differently based on what they need

- They stay calm under pressure and help their players stay calm too

- They care about their players as people, not just as athletes

10.2 Mentors Who Changed Everything

Sometimes the most important person in a player's journey isn't their official coach, it's someone who takes extra time to help them grow. These mentors become like a soccer family.

Thierry Henry and Kylian Mbappé: Passing on Greatness

When **Kylian Mbappé** was just *thirteen* years old, he met his hero **Thierry Henry** at a soccer camp. Henry was already a legend, but he took time to work with this skinny kid from Paris who dreamed of playing for France.

Henry saw something special in Mbappé's speed and intelligence, but more importantly, he saw a young player who was hungry to learn. He spent extra time with Mbappé, teaching him not just how to score goals, but how to read the game and make smart decisions.

Years later, when Mbappé scored a hat-trick in the **2022 World Cup final**, he pointed to the stands where Henry was watching. Even though Henry was now a coach for another team, that moment showed the lasting bond between mentor and student.

Henry always told Mbappé, "*Talent gets you noticed, but character keeps you at the top.*" That lesson helped Mbappé become not just a great player, but a leader who helps his teammates too.

Christine Sinclair and Jessie Fleming: Passing the Captain's Band

When **Jessie Fleming** first joined the **Canadian Women's National Team** as a teenager, she was intimidated by playing alongside **Christine Sinclair**, the same legend we met earlier who broke every goal-scoring record in the book.

But Sinclair, who had been Canada's captain and inspiration for over two decades, took Fleming under her wing. As Sinclair got older, she adapted her playing style and her role within the team, mentoring young players and offering an inspirational spark that only someone of her pedigree could provide.

During Canada's historic Olympic gold medal run in 2021, it was Fleming who stepped up to take the penalty kicks in crucial moments, including the game-tying goal in the final against Sweden. But it was Sinclair who won that penalty, showing how the veteran set up the younger player for success.

After games, Sinclair would encourage Fleming and other young players to be themselves and play their own style, showing them that every player brings something unique to the team. Sinclair has said:

"I pride myself on the impact I can have on younger players."

This mentorship spirit continues with players like **Jordyn Huitema**, who considers Sinclair her *"idol"* and represents the next generation of Canadian soccer stars.

Ronaldinho and Neymar: The Joy Connection

When **Neymar** was a teenager at Barcelona, he was incredibly talented but sometimes tried too hard to impress everyone. **Ronaldinho**, the Brazilian legend known for his smile and creativity, became his mentor.

Ronaldinho's philosophy was simple. As he once said,

"Football is about joy. It's about dribbling. I favour every idea that makes the game beautiful."

He taught Neymar that the best players are the ones who love what they do so much that it shows in every touch of the ball.

During training, Ronaldinho would show Neymar tricks and skills, but always with a big grin on his face. He helped Neymar understand that being creative and having fun wasn't selfish. It was what made soccer beautiful. Years later, Neymar would carry this lesson with him, understanding that the greatest players are those who never lose their love for the game.

From Ronaldinho to Neymar to the next generation of Brazilian stars, the message stays the same: *play with joy*, and the beautiful game becomes even more beautiful.

10.3 Parents: The Ultimate Cheerleaders

Behind every young soccer player, there's usually parents who believe in their dreams, even when those dreams seem impossible.

The Messi Family: Never Giving Up

In Chapter 3, you learned how **Lionel Messi** points to the sky after scoring, his special way of honoring the grandmother who believed in him first. But she wasn't the only one. Messi's whole family helped him chase a dream that many thought was out of reach.

You already know about Messi's growth hormone challenge when he was eleven. What you might not know is how his entire family rallied around him during those difficult years. He was smaller than the other kids, and the medicine to help him grow was very expensive. Local teams in Argentina admired his talent, but none could afford to cover the treatment.

That didn't stop his parents. His dad, **Jorge**, worked extra hours at a steel factory to pay for the shots. His mom**, Celia,** supported him at every turn and reminded him to stay focused on what he loved most, soccer. His siblings cheered him on, even as the journey became more difficult.

Then came an incredible opportunity. FC Barcelona invited Messi to Spain for a trial. If he joined their youth academy, they would help pay for his treatments. So Messi and his father packed their bags and moved to a new country, far away from everything they knew. It wasn't easy. Messi was shy, homesick, and missed his family deeply.

But his father stayed by his side. And from back home in Argentina, his family kept sending him encouragement. They believed in him, even when he doubted himself.

Today, Messi still says his family's love and support made all the difference. Every time he points to the sky after a goal, it's not just for his grandmother. It's for all the people who helped him believe that a small boy from Rosario could grow into one of the greatest players of all time.

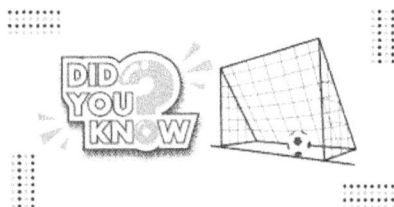

Both of Lionel Messi's biggest supporters were named **Celia**!

- His grandmother, **Celia Oliveira Cuccittini**, was the first to believe in him. She took little Messi to his soccer games and told everyone, "He's going to be a star!"

- Later, his mother, **Celia María Cuccittini**, helped him stay focused and supported him through every challenge.

Two Celias, one dream — and a soccer legend was born!

The Vieira da Silva Family: Strength Behind the Star

In Chapter 5.1, you discovered how **Marta** dazzled the world with her unstoppable footwork and became Brazil's all-time leading goal scorer, even surpassing Pelé. But behind her rise from dusty streets to soccer royalty was someone who never made the headlines: her mother, **Tereza**.

Marta grew up in Dois Riachos, a small town where people believed soccer was only for boys. She didn't have cleats or uniforms, just raw talent and a big dream. Many adults told her to stop playing. But not her mom. Tereza always told her, *"Don't listen to them. Just play."*

That quiet encouragement changed everything.

As Marta practiced on sidewalks and dirt patches, her mother supported her every step. When others laughed or doubted, her mom stood firm. When Marta had to leave home for a chance to play professionally, Tereza didn't hold her back. She hugged her daughter tight and let her go, knowing that the world needed to see what Marta could do.

Years later, after scoring goal after goal and winning award after award, Marta looked back and said,

"My mom gave me strength. She gave me everything."

Marta's story isn't just about a girl who became the **Queen of Soccer**. It's also about a mother who believed so deeply in her daughter's dream that she helped it take flight.

The Pulisic Family: Chasing Dreams Across Oceans

Christian Pulisic's parents, **Mark** and **Kelley**, made a huge sacrifice for their son's soccer dreams. When Christian was just sixteen, he had a chance to join **Borussia Dortmund**'s academy in **Germany**, but it meant leaving his family behind.

Instead of holding him back out of fear, his parents encouraged him to take the chance. His father **Mark** has said they never put pressure on Christian and even almost pushed him in directions other than soccer to make sure it was truly his choice.

His parents were so protective of his love for the game that they even removed him from teams where coaches were too negative or had big egos. They understood that keeping soccer fun was more important than being on the "best" team.

For two years, Christian lived in Germany while his parents stayed in Pennsylvania, supporting him through video calls and care packages. When he achieved his dreams of playing professional soccer, he knew his parents' support had made it possible.

The Pulisic family shows us something important: the best soccer parents don't just cheer from the sidelines. They protect their children's dreams, even when those dreams take them far from home. They teach that loving the game matters more than winning every match, and that sometimes the biggest act of love is letting your child chase their dreams across an ocean.

10.4 Who Inspires You?

While these famous stories of coaches, mentors, and families are incredible, the truth is that every soccer player has their own unique support network. Your coaches might not be household names, your mentors might be teammates or neighbors, and your family's story might be completely different from the ones we've shared and that's what makes your journey special.

Your Personal Soccer Family

Think about the people in your own soccer story. Who taught you your first skill? Who cheers the loudest when you play? Who helps you practice in the backyard when you want to get better? Who makes you laugh when you're feeling nervous before a big game? Who reminds you that trying your best is what matters most?

These people might not be famous coaches or legendary players, but they're the most important people in your soccer journey. They deserve to be celebrated just as much as any superstar.

Sometimes we forget to tell the important people in our lives how much they mean to us. Your coach who stays after practice to help you with headers. Your parents who drive you to early morning games. Your older teammate who shows you how to take better corner kicks. Your friend who always passes you the ball even when they could score themselves. They all make your soccer dreams possible.

Becoming Someone's Hero

Here's a secret: you don't have to be a professional player to inspire someone else. Maybe there's a younger kid on your team who watches everything you do. Maybe there's a friend who's nervous about trying soccer for the first time. Maybe there's a teammate who's having a tough game and needs encouragement.

You have the power to be someone's positive influence. When you include new players and make them feel welcome, when you stay positive during tough games, when you share what you've learned with someone who's struggling, you're being the kind of person others look up to.

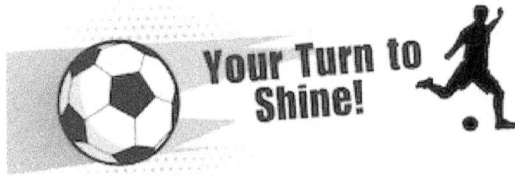

Inspiration Action Challenge:

Create Your Support Team Trading Cards:
1. Make a trading card for each important person in your soccer journey.

2. Include their "special powers" (like "Always knows what to say" or "Makes the best post-game snacks").

3. Write one thing they've taught you on the back.

4. Keep these cards as reminders of how lucky you are to have such an amazing team supporting you.

The Gratitude Goal: This week, tell one person from your support team specifically how they've helped you. Watch how much it means to them, and how good it makes you feel too!

The circle of support never ends. From legendary coaches to devoted parents, from inspiring mentors to teammates who become family, every great player's story is really the story of everyone who believed in them along the way. And now, as we reach the end of our journey together, it's time to think about your place in soccer's incredible story.

The Circle Continues

As you continue your soccer journey, you'll meet more coaches, mentors, and teammates who will help shape who you become. Some will teach you new skills. Others will help you through difficult times. A few might become lifelong friends. All of them will be part of your soccer story, and you'll be part of theirs.

The greatest players in the world all have stories about people who believed in them, guided them, and supported them. But remember, you're not just someone who receives support. Every time you encourage a teammate, help a younger player, or simply show good sportsmanship, you're continuing the circle of support that makes soccer so special.

From legendary coaches to devoted parents, from inspiring mentors to teammates who become family, every great player's story is really the story of everyone who believed in them along the way. And now it's time to think about your place in soccer's incredible story.

Chapter 11: Behind the Scenes in a World Cup City

"It's not just a game. It's the world coming together, and every host city gets ready to welcome them all."

Have you ever wondered what it takes to transform an ordinary city into a **World Cup** host? How do they prepare for the greatest soccer tournament on Earth? When the FIFA **World Cup comes to North America in 2026**, cities like **New York, Mexico City, Vancouver,** and **Toronto** will roll out the green carpet for the most amazing players and passionate fans on the planet.

But here's the incredible part: turning a regular city into a World Cup host isn't just about painting some lines on a field. It's like preparing for the biggest, most exciting party the world has ever seen!

I discovered this firsthand when my friend Mike, who worked as a network engineer on BMO Field's World Cup upgrades, showed me what really went on behind the scenes. *"Want to see how we prepared to welcome the world?"* he asked with a huge grin. How could I say no?

11.1 Stepping Into a Stadium of the Future

BMO Field sits right on **Toronto**'s gorgeous waterfront, where you can smell the lake breeze and see the CN Tower reaching up to the clouds. On any regular day, it's an awesome place to watch **Toronto FC** battle their rivals or cheer for the **Canadian women's national team**. But for the World Cup? Everything has to be absolutely perfect.

As we entered through Gate 5, close to the players' entrance, Mike explained the incredible transformation happening all around us. *"We didn't just fix up a stadium,"* he said as we walked through what looked like the world's most organized construction site. *"We built a place where dreams come true."*

That's when we met Sam, the field technician who has access to all the stadium's facilities and equipment. With his expert knowledge of every corner of BMO Field, Sam would show us areas that most people never get to see.

The first thing that amazed me was the size of everything. Temporary seating had boosted the stadium from 28,000 seats to 45,000. That's like adding an entire high school to the crowd! But it wasn't just about cramming in more people. Every single seat had to have a perfect view of the field, easy access to bathrooms and food, and super-fast Wi-Fi so fans could share their excitement with friends around the world.

BIGGER STADIUM, BIGGER CONNECTIONS

More than 45,000 fans will cheer here – so the stadium is adding thousands of new seats and more internet connections!

As Sam led us into the executive suites, Mike showed me the network infrastructure that makes everything possible. We could see antennas and WiFi access points strategically placed throughout the stadium. *"These connect our systems to practically every part of the facility,"* Mike explained, pointing to the sophisticated setup. *"When millions of people around the world are watching, everything has to work perfectly."*

STAYING CONNECTED - HOW NETWORK KEEPS UP

Rounded "puck" DAS Antenna

This rectangular antenna focuses 4G and 5G into a specific section, like a spotlight, which boosts capacity for the crowd.

This small ceiling antenna spreads cellular signal evenly in this room so nearby phones stay connected.

Directional Cellular Panel Antenna

The Super-Tech Soccer Stadium

Here's something that might surprise you: a World Cup stadium needs to be like a giant computer that also happens to have a soccer field in the middle! When 45,000 fans show up to watch their heroes play, they're not just watching. They're taking pictures, posting videos, texting their friends, and streaming highlights. That means the stadium needs more internet power than most small towns!

What We Saw on Our Behind-the-Scenes Tour

Mike got excited showing us the network upgrades. *"Look at these sectors and antennas,"* he said, pointing to directional antennas, RF equipment, and fiber optic cables positioned throughout the stadium. *"Each sector can handle thousands of people uploading their World Cup memories at the same time."*

STAYING CONNECTED - HOW NETWORK KEEPS UP

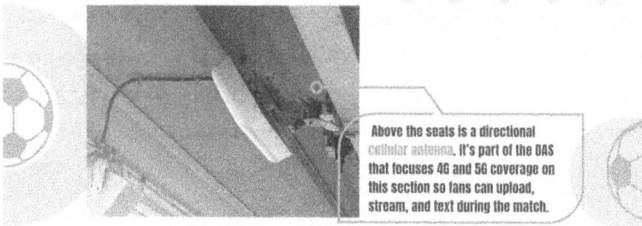

Above the seats is a directional cellular antenna. It's part of the DAS that focuses 4G and 5G coverage on this section so fans can upload, stream, and text during the match.

Cellular Antenna (DAS - Distributed Antenna System)

STAYING CONNECTED - HOW NETWORK KEEPS UP

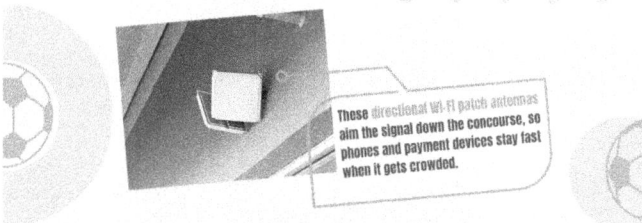

These directional Wi-Fi patch antennas aim the signal down the concourse, so phones and payment devices stay fast when it gets crowded.

From super antennas on the ceiling to Wi-Fi panels in the corners – everything is getting smarter and faster so fans can stay online during the action!

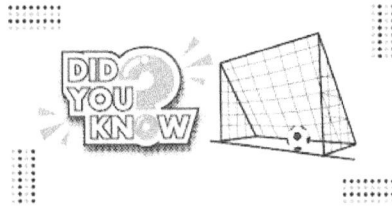

To get **BMO Field** ready for the **2026 World Cup**, engineers didn't just add more seats (from 28,000 to 45,000 fans) — they also boosted the cellular signal so everyone's phones could work during the big games!

But how do they do that?
They slice the stadium into invisible "sectors", kind of like pizza slices. Each "slice" or sector has its own antenna that helps fans stay connected.

Tech Pizza Time!
Each sector can handle around **1,500 to 2,000 fans** sending texts, photos, and videos. So for 45,000 fans, the stadium might need about **23 to 30 sectors** — that's a lot of slices!

Just like each slice holds different toppings, each sector handles its own chunk of wireless traffic. Thanks to smart planning, your messages go through—even in a crowd!

We also saw the outdoor cellular antennas that had been added. *"Safety is super important with antennas,"* Mike noted. *"We have to make sure they're positioned so they don't harm anyone while still providing fast and reliable coverage."*

STAYING CONNECTED – OUTDOOR CELLULAR SECTORS

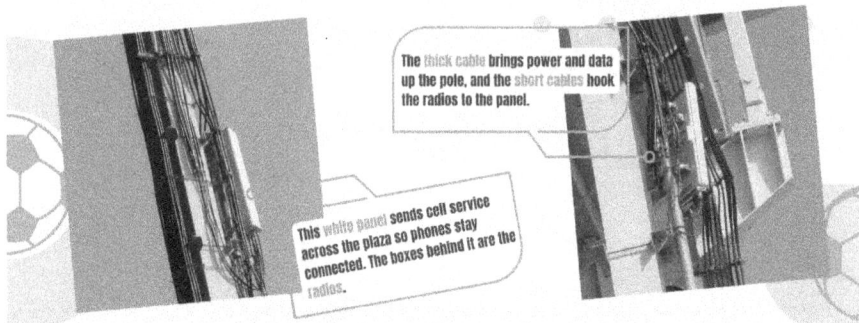

The thick cable brings power and data up the pole, and the short cables hook the radios to the panel.

This white panel sends cell service across the plaza so phones stay connected. The boxes behind it are the radios.

Even before you enter the stadium, tech towers help your phone connect. You might not see them – but they're working hard!

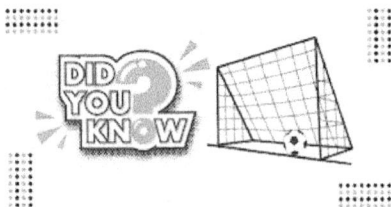

Cellular antennas help fans stream, post, and message during big games — even in packed stadiums!

At places like BMO Field, engineers carefully place antennas high up so people stay safe while getting great coverage. They even wear special gear and sometimes turn off antennas during maintenance. Safety always comes first — even for signals in the sky!

Have you ever spotted one of these antennas at a game or concert?

Sam then took us to the media room, where high-zoom cameras and broadcasting equipment were set up for journalists from around the world. *"This is where the magic happens for TV viewers everywhere,"* he explained.

The coolest part was touring the players' areas. We saw Toronto FC's locker room, complete with an exercise room and sauna. Sam showed us both Toronto FC's facilities and Soccer Canada's players' lockers, where national team heroes would prepare for their biggest matches.

Finally, we made it down to the lowest level, right at the front and center of the field. The grass had been completely replaced to meet FIFA's strict requirements, and everything was spotlessly clean, ready for the world's best players.

The FIFA Checklist: Making Everything Perfect

You might think FIFA just picks the biggest stadium and calls it good, but it's way more complicated than that. Sam enumerated a checklist that seemed longer than math homework! FIFA has specific rules for everything: how bright the lights need to be, how big the locker rooms must be, where cameras can go, how quickly emergency teams can respond, and even how garbage gets collected during games.

"We didn't have to start from zero," Sam explained as we walked through different areas. "We used what was already here and made it way better. It's like upgrading your video game console instead of buying a whole new one!"

The field itself has to be perfect too. The exact right size, with grass that's the perfect height and color. Even the goals have to meet special FIFA standards. Sam showed us where they had replaced the entire field surface to meet FIFA's strict requirements. Nothing is left to chance when the whole world is watching.

"FIFA has requirements for absolutely everything," Sam continued, "including quiet zones where players can focus, special testing areas for anti-doping, and dedicated pathways so camera operators don't bump into each other."

We also visited an executive suite where Sam showed us TVs displaying real-time game statistics and data. "During matches, this is where officials and VIPs can monitor everything that's happening," he explained.

As we finished exploring the technical marvels, Mike grinned. "But you know what? All this amazing technology is just the beginning. Wait until you see how the entire city transforms to welcome the world."

11.2 When the World Comes to Your City

Now that you've seen how a stadium transforms into a high-tech soccer temple, let me show you something even more incredible: how an entire city becomes the world's biggest neighborhood party.

Here's what makes a diverse World Cup host city like Toronto extra special: it becomes like having 32 different hometown crowds all in one place! Toronto is one of the most diverse cities on Earth, which means when the World Cup arrives, practically every team playing already has fans living there.

Little Portugal gets covered in Portuguese flags and fills with the smell of amazing food. **Chinatown** buzzes with excitement for Asian teams. **Greektown** echoes with chants and songs. **Little Jamaica** turns into a festival of music and celebration. It's like the whole world moved to one city!

Schools across the city organize special **World Cup weeks**. Kids learn about the geography of competing countries, practice different languages, and organize their own mini-tournaments. Some lucky students get to interview real players as junior reporters, while others become youth ambassadors at fan parks where families can play soccer, try virtual reality games, and learn about cultures from around the world.

Even the **subway system** gets transformed! Station signs are updated with FIFA branding and multiple languages. Friendly **volunteers** in bright World Cup jerseys greet fans at major stations, helping visitors navigate the city and sharing information about matches. Platform screens display soccer highlights and fan celebrations from around the world.

The Real Heroes: People Making Dreams Happen

But here's what I realized as Mike and I explored the stadium: behind all this amazing technology are thousands of ordinary people doing extraordinary things. Engineers like Mike work hard to make sure the network is right-sized and stable. Volunteers are signing up from all over the city, excited to contribute to this big event. Artists create beautiful decorations that welcome the world to Toronto.

There are people training ball kids who will retrieve soccer balls during games (and probably become the most envious kids in Canada!). Security teams practice how to keep everyone safe while still making sure the atmosphere stays fun and exciting. Even mascot performers rehearse their dance moves!

What struck me most was how excited everyone seemed. These aren't just people doing jobs—they're people helping create something magical that will be remembered forever.

11.3 Where Dreams Take the Field

As our tour ended, Mike and I walked to the center circle of the field. The stadium was quiet except for the distant sounds of construction, but it felt full of possibility.

"Right here," Mike said, pointing to the spot where we stood, *"is where penalty shootouts will be decided. Where last-minute goals will send fans into celebration. Where players will cry tears of joy and disappointment. Where moments that people will talk about for the rest of their lives will unfold."*

It's incredible to think that during the World Cup, this peaceful spot becomes the center of global attention, where soccer history gets written. Every four years, a new city gets to be the stage where dreams come true.

What This Means for Kids Like You

As we stood in the middle of the empty field, Mike asked me something that gave me goosebumps: *"Can you imagine what it will feel like when this place is packed with 45,000 people all cheering at the same time?"*

I looked around at the empty seats and tried to picture it: fans wearing jerseys from every corner of the world, flags waving, songs echoing through the stadium, and the world's best players running on this very grass beneath our feet.

"The coolest part," Mike continued, *"is that kids in Toronto got to see their heroes play in person. Not on TV, not on YouTube, but right here in their own*

city. Some of those kids might decide that day that they want to become professional players. Others might realize they want to become engineers like me, field technicians like Sam, or event planners, or sports journalists."

The World Cup is so much more than just watching 32 teams play soccer. It's like a giant spotlight that shines on kids everywhere, showing them that their biggest dreams can come true too!

And here's the coolest secret of all: you don't need to be the next Messi or Ronaldo to be part of World Cup magic! Think about it—without Mike making sure every WiFi signal reaches the stands, fans couldn't share their excitement with friends back home. Without Sam checking that every camera angle is perfect, kids around the world couldn't watch their heroes score incredible goals. These behind-the-scenes champions are just as important as the players on the field, proving that there are a million different ways to help create moments the whole world will never forget!

I couldn't be more proud of Mike and Sam for their amazing contributions—not just to our community, but to soccer history. They're the kind of unsung heroes who work quietly behind the scenes, making big dreams come true for everyone. Whether it's making sure the stadium Wi-Fi works or capturing every perfect goal on camera, they help create the magic of the World Cup in ways most people never see.

Meet the Real-Life Heroes

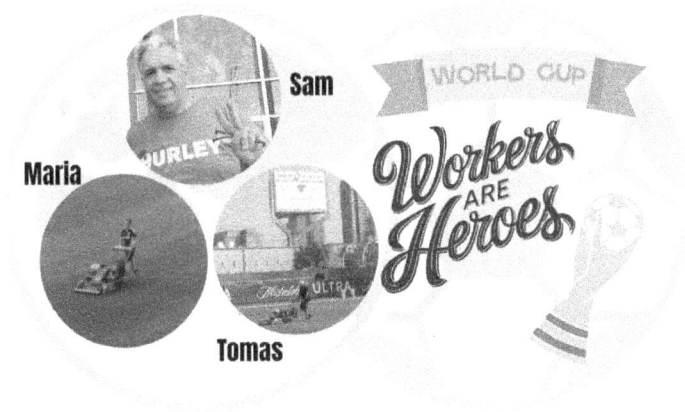

This eBook includes exclusive behind-the-scenes photos from BMO Field — where a dedicated team of everyday heroes helps make World Cup magic possible!

Mike – The Signal Superhero
Mike is a telecom engineer who helped upgrade BMO Field so fans could share every cheer, goal, and celebration—without missing a single signal! He makes sure Wi-Fi and cellular networks work smoothly, even with tens of thousands of fans using their phones at the same time. Talk about super skills!

Sam – The Field Fixer
Sam is a field technician who checks all the cables, antennas, and connections around the stadium. If anything isn't working right, Sam is the one who climbs, adjusts, and fixes it—fast! Thanks to Sam, the tech behind the scenes stays strong all game long.

Maria & Tomas – The Grass Guardians
Maria and Tomas help care for the pitch—the grassy field where all the action happens. With early morning starts and expert tools, they keep the turf smooth, safe, and game-day ready. Without their hard work, world-class soccer wouldn't look (or feel!) the same.

They're not just workers—they're hometown heroes! Thanks to this amazing team, the World Cup isn't just magical—it's possible.

FUN FACT

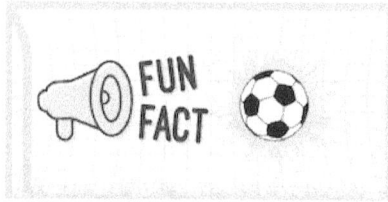

KEY UPGRADES AT BMO FIELD FOR WORLD CUP 2026

So what exactly got upgraded? Check out these stadium superpowers!

1 Expanded Seating - Temporary seats boost capacity from about 28,000 to 45,000.

2 Stronger Wi-Fi & Faster Concessions - Upgraded Wi-Fi and more self-serve tech at snack stands.

3 Brighter Lights & Video Boards - Four new LED screens and improved stadium lighting and sound.

4 Media & Broadcasting Enhancements - Better equipment zones for global TV and streaming coverage.

5 New Bathrooms & Food Stalls - More fan-friendly areas for comfort on game day.

6 Safety & Accessibility Upgrades - Better exits, ramps, and safety systems for bigger crowds.

7 Upgraded Player Areas - Improved locker rooms, dugouts, and team zones.

8 Greener Choices - Eco-friendly materials and sustainable systems.

Are you curious to explore even more photos, videos, and fun facts about how a real stadium prepares for the **FIFA World Cup 2026**? Scan this QR code or visit *https://tinyurl.com/54zmvecv* to go behind the scenes at Toronto's BMO Field — a real host venue!

The Magic of Coming Together

As Mike and I headed back to the parking lot, the morning sun was getting warmer and the construction site buzzed with activity. That's when something powerful hit me about everything we'd just experienced.

You don't need to wait for the World Cup to start making this same kind of magic happen. Every time you welcome a new kid into your soccer game, cheer extra loud for a teammate, or show awesome sportsmanship even when you're losing, you're creating the exact same spirit that makes the World Cup so special.

The excitement. The teamwork. The joy of bringing people together. It all starts with you, right where you are, with whatever ball you have and whoever wants to play.

So next time you kick a ball, remember this: you're not just playing a game. You're part of a story that connects you to kids speaking every language, living in every country, all sharing the same incredible dream.

And who knows? Maybe one day, you'll be the one standing in that center circle, ready to make World Cup history of your own.

Special Thanks
*I'm grateful to **Mike** and **Sam**, who guided me through hidden areas of BMO Field and shared real stories about how the stadium gets ready for big events. Their insights helped bring this chapter to life.*

CONCLUSION

Hey there! Can you believe we've made it to the end of this soccer adventure? We've traveled through time, from ancient China's *Cuju* to modern-day stadiums buzzing with excitement. Soccer's more than just what happens on the pitch. It carries stories, struggles, and the spirit of the people who play it.

We've met legends like *Messi* and *Ronaldo*. Their stories teach us about humility, dedication, and perseverance. They didn't just kick a ball. They kicked down barriers and showed us how far passion can take you. Then there are modern heroes like *Mbappé* and *Morgan*. They're showing us what it means to shine on and off the field. Their influence goes beyond trophies. They inspire us to dream bigger and aim higher.

Let's not forget the rising stars and incredible women blazing trails in soccer. These players show us that with determination, anything is possible. We've seen how soccer empowers girls and welcomes everyone onto the field. It's about breaking barriers and chasing dreams.

Soccer teaches us life skills that stick with us. *Resilience, teamwork, confidence,* and *sportsmanship* are just a few of the lessons we've learned. Whether it's bouncing back from a loss or cheering for a teammate, soccer mirrors the ups and downs of life.

The global reach of soccer is something to celebrate. It's incredible how a simple game unites people from all walks of life. We've shared iconic moments that inspired generations. And we've had plenty of laughs along the way because soccer is also about having fun.

Mentors, coaches, and *family* play vital roles in nurturing talent. They guide us, believe in us, and help us grow. They're the unsung heroes who make dreams possible. Their wisdom and encouragement light the way.

I'll never forget watching the 2022 World Cup Final from a giant screen with in that Cuban resort. The warm breeze drifted in as families, kids, and travelers from every corner of the globe gathered around one glowing screen. When Lionel Messi finally lifted the World Cup trophy—after years of heartbreak and near-misses—the room erupted. Cheers, hugs, even tears. I couldn't help but smile. That moment reminded me: *some dreams take time, but they're worth fighting for.*

Messi never gave up, and neither should you.

Soccer's messy. You fall, you miss, you yell, you laugh. But you keep going, and that's the part that sticks. It's about heart, effort, and the courage to try again. It brings people together, strangers on a beach, teammates on a field, fans across continents, reminding us we're part of something bigger.

And now, it's your turn.

Wherever you are, whatever your dream is, remember this: Every soccer legend was once just a kid with a ball, just like you.

So, go imagine. Go play. Go write your story.

Because your biggest moment might be just one kick away.

Also by Dylan Ambrose

Thanks for picking up *Epic Soccer Stories*! I hope these tales inspired you to dream big, play bold, and believe in your journey—on and off the field.

Love epic sports stories?

The action doesn't stop here. Every sport has its legends, its unforgettable moments, and its heroes who refused to quit. Whether you're into basketball, baseball, or beyond—there's an epic adventure waiting for you.

Epic Sports Series (Ages 8–12):

- *Epic Basketball Stories*

- *Epic Soccer Stories*

- Coming Soon: Baseball, Football, Hockey, Tennis, and Golf

Activity Books:

- *Epic Basketball Activity Book*

- Coming Soon: Soccer, Baseball, and more

Ready for your next challenge?

Head to **https://yearnmorebooks.com/Books/** for exclusive bonuses, sneak peeks, and the full Epic Sports collection or simply scan the QR code.

To your next adventure,
Dylan Ambrose
Epic Sports for Kids | YearnMoreBooks.com

REFERENCES

Origins: Pre-Histories of Football https://www.fifamuseum.com/en/exhibitions-and-events/exhibitions/editorials-and-virtuals-exhibitions/origins-pre-histories-of-football

Football (soccer) | History, Game, Rules, & Significant Players https://www.britannica.com/sports/football-soccer

Pelé https://en.wikipedia.org/wiki/Pele

_An unknown story - the 1921 ban on women's football https://thefsa.org.uk/news/an-untold-story-the-1921-ban-on-womens-football/

The 5 Most Iconic Moments Of Diego Maradona's Career https://www.forbes.com/sites/robertkidd/2020/11/27/the-5-most-iconic-moments-of-diego-maradonas-career/

Famous for Hot Moment, Zinedine Zidane is Cool as a Coach https://www.nytimes.com/2016/04/17/sports/soccer/famous-for-hot-moment-zinedine-zidaneis-cool-as-a-coach.html

Christine Sinclair uses philanthropy to break down gender ... https://www.vancouverfoundation.ca/donor-stories/how-christine-sinclair-is-using-philanthropy-to-break-down-gender-barriers-in-sport/

Lionel Messi: Overcoming Adversity to Achieve Greatness! https://vocal.media/motivation/lionel-messi-overcoming-adversity-to-achieve-greatness#:~:text=Messi's%20family%20struggled%20to%20make,improvised%20balls%20made%20from%20rags.

The Tiger Mentality: How Cristiano Ronaldo's Work Ethic Has ... https://4pballer.com/the-tiger-mentality-how-cristiano-ronaldos-work-e thic-has-helped-him-achieve-greatness/#:~:text=Consistently%20pushin g%20himself%20to%20new,opportunity%20to%20learn%20and%20gro w.

Kylian   Mbappé   -   Wikipedia https://en.wikipedia.org/wiki/Kylian_Mbapp%C3%A9#:~:text=He%20als o%20helped%20France%20to,by%20scoring%20a%20hat%2Dtrick.

Alex Morgan: A Legacy of Excellence - EnforceTheSport.com https://www .enforcethesport.com/blog/alex-morgan-a-legacy-of-excellence

Jude   Bellingham: The   20-year-old   leading   by   exam-ple https://fifpro.org/en/supporting-players/player-influence/world11/j ude-bellingham-leading-by-example-at-age-20

Alphonso   Davies'   journey: from   a   refugee   camp   to   world ... https://www.bundesliga.com/en/bundesliga/news/alphonso-davies-f rom-refugee-to-bayern-munich-canada-world-cup-1239

VIDEO: Jadon   Sancho   Reveals   'Justice   for   George   Floyd' ... https://www.businessinsider.com/video-jadon-sancho-hat-trick-geor ge-floyd-shirt-2020-5

Trinity   Rodman's   soccer   titles: USWNT,   NWSL   awards   and ... https://www.espn.com/soccer/story/_/id/40624470/trinity-rodman-s occer-career-honors-awards-more-stats

Marta   Da   Silva | Biography,   Competitions,   Wins   and   Medals https://www.olympics.com/en/athletes/marta#:~:text=Marta%20Vieira% 20da%20Silva%2C%20known,women's%20team%20at%20just%2014.

Ada Hegerberg: Leading the Charge for Equality and ... https://beyondth epitch24.substack.com/p/ada-hegerberg-leading-the-charge

Sam   Kerr   -   Wikipedia https://en.wikipedia.org/wiki/Sam_Kerr#:~:text=Kerr%20is%20the%20al l%2Dtime,the%20United%20States%20until%202024.

How   Nigeria's   Asisat   Oshoala   leads   on   and   off   the   pitch ... https://www.olympics.com/en/news/nigeria-asisat-oshoala-leader-fo otball-paris-2024-olympics

From Cancer to Glory: The Inspiring Journey of Linda Caicedo https://8lete.life/stories/footballer-linda-caicedo#:~:text=She%20de buted%20professionally%20at%20the,her%20career%20might%20e nd%20prematurely.

FC Barcelona 6–1 Paris Saint-Germain FC - Wikipedia https://en.wikipedia.org/wiki/FC_Barcelona_6%E2%80%931_Paris_ Saint-Germain_FC#:~:text=Barcelona%20overcame%20a%20four%2 Dgoal,(the%20comeback%3B%20Catalan%3A%20La

Cristiano Ronaldo on his rivalry with Lionel Messi https://www.indiatoday.in/sports/football/story/cristiano-ronaldo-o n-his-rivalry-with-lionel-messi-we-are-not-friends-but-we-respect-ea ch-other-2432118-2023-09-07

Paolo Di Canio https://en.wikipedia.org/wiki/Paolo_Di_Canio

Soccer's Global Impact: How the Sport Influences Economies ... https://www.marygrovemustangs.com/soccers-global-impact-how-t he-sport-influences-economies-and-cultures.html#:~:text=and%20ec onomic%20diversification.-,Soccer%20as%20a%20Cultural%20Unifi er%20and%20Divider,of%20community%20and%20national%20ide ntity.

World Cup | History & Winners https://www.britannica.com/sports/W orld-Cup-football

How Nelson Mandela Used Rugby as a Symbol of South ... https://www.history.com/articles/nelson-mandela-1995-rugby-w orld-cup-south-african-unity

Didier Drogba: How Ivory Coast striker helped to halt civil ... https:// www.bbc.com/sport/football/52072592

The Times 50 Greatest Football Matches https://thehistorypress.co.u k/publication/the-times-50-greatest-football-matches/

Liverpool vs. AC Milan: 'Something unreal happened' in ... https://www.cnn.com/2020/05/22/football/liverpool-ac-milan-ch ampions-league-final-istanbul-cmd-spt-intl

The hand of God https://en.wikipedia.org/wiki/The_hand_of_God

FIFA Council confirms Women's World Cup expansion https://www.fifa.com/en/articles/fifa-council-womens-world-cup-expansion

The most iconic goal celebrations https://www.fourfourtwo.com/features/the-most-iconic-goal-celebrations

Development and Initial Validation of the Humor Climate in ... https://pmc.ncbi.nlm.nih.gov/articles/PMC8360852/

The Crucial Role of Youth Soccer Coach Education https://www.bottlenoses.com/article-blog/protecting-young-athletes-the-crucial-role-of-coach-certification-and-education-r9n4k-jttny-kyb6f?srsltid=AfmBOorZCLJ9TBc_baPPkaWD8F7auZC23O__Rsy8CjVu-lCXcxTg69Rr

6 Mentors of the World's Biggest Superstars https://www.si.com/soccer/2019/02/11/6-mentors-worlds-biggest-superstars

The Role of Parental Involvement in Youth Sport Experience https://pmc.ncbi.nlm.nih.gov/articles/PMC8391271/

Characteristics of an Effective Soccer Coach https://www.rpbstrikers.com/recreation/characteristics-of-an-effective-soccer-coach

The Impact of the FIFA World Cup on International Unity https://aithor.com/essay-examples/the-impact-of-the-fifa-world-cup-on-international-unity

Grassroot Soccer: Home https://grassrootsoccer.org/

Soccer Without Borders https://www.soccerwithoutborders.org/

Inspirational Soccer Stories https://soccernation.com/category/inspiration/

Drogba, D. (2007, July 30). *Didier Drogba: The Peacekeeper*. Time. https://content.time.com/time/magazine/article/0,9171,1649286,00.html.

Evans, D. K. (2015). Global Game, Local Identity: The Social Production of Football Space in Liverpool.

The Impact of International Soccer Broadcast on Fans | TeteZo News. https://tetezonews.com/25515-the-impact-of-international-soccer-broadcast-on-fans-41/

Premier League. (2012, May 13). *Manchester City 3–2 QPR match report.* https://www.premierleague.com/...

France Football. (2020, September). *Sadio Mané: "I don't need luxury. I prefer that my people get a little of what life has given me."* [Interview]. Reprinted in Goal.com . https://www.goal.com/en/news/i-dont-need-10-ferraris-mane-on-hel ping-his-people-and/1b1pnh6a2k0q1tj3u16k7gmld

Ibrahim, M. (2022, April 26). *The incredible generosity of Sadio Mané: Donations, schools, and hospitals.* The Daily Mail. https://www.dailymai l.co.uk/sport/football/article-10754631

Ahmed, S. (2023, July 5). OPINION | With a newfound roar in her voice, Canada's Sinclair readies for a 6th Women's World Cup. *CBC Sports.* https://www.cbc.ca/sports/opinion-women-world-cup-christin e-sinclair-shireen-ahmed-1.6895309

Christine Sinclair. (2025, January 29). In *Wikipedia.* https://en.wikipedia .org/wiki/Christine_Sinclair

For Jordyn Huitema considering Sinclair her "idol":

Seven key moments Canada and PSG star Jordyn Huitema has blazed her own trail. (2025, January 27). *Olympics.com.* https://www.olympics.com /en/news/jordyn-huitema-psg-canada-trailblazing

Tognini, G. (2021, June 23). *The humble superstar: Why Sadio Mané gives back to Senegal.* Forbes Africa. https://www.forbesafrica.com/life/2021 /06/23/the-humble-superstar-sadio-mane-gives-back-to-senegal/

Ruiz, D. (2023, October 10). The philosophy behind Ronaldinho's joyful football. *Tribuna.com.* https://www.tribuna.com/en/news/realmadrid-2 023-10-10-the-philosophy-behind-ronaldinhos-joyful-football/

FIFA. (2018, March 19). *Marta: The voice of women's football.* FIFA.com . https://www.fifa.com/news/marta-the-voice-of-womens-football-291 1072

Borden, S. (2015, June 11). Marta of Brazil, soccer star with enduring pow-er. *The New York Times.* https://www.nytimes.com/2015/06/12/sports/s occer/world-cup-marta-of-brazil-soccer-star-with-enduring-power.html

FIFA. (2022, June 16). FIFA World Cup 2026™ host cities announced. FIFA.com. https://www.fifa.com/tournaments/mens/worldcup/canadamexicousa2026/media-releases/fifa-world-cup-2026-tm-host-cities-announced

France Football. (2020). *Ballon d'Or: Le palmarès complet depuis 1956* [Ballon d'Or: Complete list of winners since 1956]. France Football. https://www.francefootball.fr/news/Ballon-d-or-le-palmares-complet/423058

FIFA. (1970). *1970 FIFA World Cup Mexico: Official report*. Fédération Internationale de Football Association.

Goldblatt, D. (2006). *The ball is round: A global history of soccer*. Riverhead Books.

Premier League. (2012). *Manchester City 3-2 Queens Park Rangers match report, May 13, 2012*. Premier League Official Website.

Premier League. (2016). *Leicester City: Premier League champions 2015-16 season review*. Premier League Official Website.

UEFA. (1992). *UEFA European Championship 1992: Official report*. Union of European Football Associations.

Vialli, G. (2006). *The Italian job: A journey to the heart of two great footballing cultures*. Bantam.

Viborg, J. (2012). *The miracle summer: Denmark's European Championship triumph 1992*. Gyldendal.

Wilson, J. (2013). *The anatomy of Manchester City*. Orion.

Benson, J. (2016). *5000-1: The Leicester City story*. Bonnier Books.

www.ingramcontent.com/pod-product-compliance
Lightning Source LLC
Chambersburg PA
CBHW022006090426
42741CB00007B/916